MY LIFE
AND
LESSONS

GENE VAN SHAAR

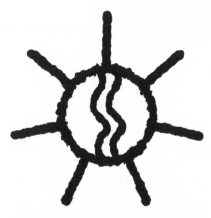

CLEAR CREEK
CANYON PRESS
ClearCreekCanyonPress.com

Printed in the United States of America

First Printing, 2016

ISBN-10: 1523961287; ISBN-13: 978-1523961283

cover and
book design by

JOURNAL
DESIGN
www.JournalDesign.com

Table of Contents

Editor's Preface

I started attending The Church of Jesus Christ of Latter-day Saints the summer before 9th grade, then found myself in early morning seminary two months later. Brother Van Shaar was my teacher and provided my introduction to the gospel of Jesus Christ. What a wonderful introduction it was!

It was fun for me to read through this manuscript for the first time, because so many of these stories stuck with me from when I was a student and became part of who I am and how I understand the gospel. That in itself is remarkable. After all, how many lessons do you remember from twenty-seven years ago?

If you were not fortunate enough to be Brother Van Shaar's student, following are a few things you could expect from his class that simply cannot be captured on the printed page.

You would expect to feel the Spirit every day. He is passionate about the gospel. Under his influence, you would become as excited about, and feel as deeply grateful for the gospel as he does.

You would laugh every day. He is impossibly funny. That, as much as the spiritual nourishment you would receive would strengthen you for the day ahead.

Your favorite classes would always be the ones where he told stories. He is a master storyteller, using his voice and body language to have you laughing, then groaning in disgust, then crying because the Spirit is so very strong.

You would come to expect miracles in your life. You would learn that they really do happen in the lives of faith-filled, but otherwise ordinary people. They come, not because we demand them, but as generous gifts from a powerful and loving God.

You would never be bored. Brother Van Shaar is a master teacher who uses a wide variety of teaching methods so that class is never the same. He has a gift for writing excellent questions that get his students engaged with the material and involved in discussion.

You would have a true friend. He would eat pizza and play pool or basketball with you. His office door would always be open to you, and you could talk to him about anything. In the seminary or institute building, you would find refuge from the cares of the world, tuck into a spiritual feast, have a good laugh, and leave better for having been there.

In this book, Gene Van Shaar has created for you an independent-study gospel course, based on his life and lessons. I hope you will really engage with the material. Look up the references. Make notes and ask questions in the margins. Each chapter ends with carefully crafted questions. Take the time to prayerfully study and answer them, and discuss them with your family. As you do so, the Spirit will whisper to your mind, and you will find "treasures of wisdom and knowledge." (Colossians 2:3)

—Diana Miles

Author's Preface and Acknowledgments

This book presents some of the most interesting things I have experienced in my life. It also includes some lessons that I have given that I hope will be enlightening. This is not meant to be a journal or an accounting of all I value in my life. It is autobiographical but it is not an autobiography. This is not the story of my family but family members are among those who appear in these chapters. I have written this with the hope that my family and friends will enjoy these stories and that they, as well as other readers, will be edified as they consider *My Life and Lessons*.

The contents of this book are true as I have perceived them, and accurate as I remember them. In order to protect privacy, most of the names of people and places have been withheld or changed.

I would like to express appreciation to the following people who generously volunteered their time to help with editing: Shelly Wallentine, Megan Wallentine, Kelly Shepherd, Tom and Shawnee Austad, Barbra Van Shaar, Kimberly Ells, Robyn Van Shaar, and a few others who prefer to remain anonymous. Several editors were actual participants in episodes that are included in this book.

Special thanks to Diana Miles for primary editing and proofreading. I saw much evidence of her inspiration in the editing process. She did major sections of amazing and revelatory re-writing that conveyed what I meant to say, but was not able to on my own.

—Gene Van Shaar

CHAPTER 1

The Meaning of the Vision

"A new and everlasting covenant…" (D&C 22:1)

I was in the mission field in Garden Grove, California in 1968. My companion and I taught a Brother Benjamin. He told us quite a bit about himself. As I recall, he was involved in both medical and business ventures. He was very intelligent, quite wealthy, and seemed to be a very good man. He told us that he was in the Philippines during World War II, and was a prisoner in the Bataan Death March. He told us that he led a successful escape from the prison camp, even though there were few who managed to escape. He felt that the Lord had blessed him and those that were with him to be able to survive and escape.

He told us that he was raised in a traditional branch of the Dutch Catholic Church. When we asked him if he was willing to be baptized, he said he could not because he had made a commitment to his church, family and community when he was a young man. He felt that being baptized into the Church of Jesus Christ of Latter-day Saints would break that commitment. In response, I read him Doctrine and Covenants, section 22, "Behold, I say unto you that all old covenants have I caused to be done away in this thing; and this is a new and an everlasting covenant, even that which was from the beginning. Wherefore, although a man should be baptized an hundred times it availeth him nothing, for you cannot enter in at the strait gate by the law of Moses, neither by your dead works. For it is because of your dead works that I have caused this last covenant and this church to be built up unto me, even as in days of old. Wherefore, enter ye in at the gate, as I have commanded, and seek not to counsel your God. Amen." He was very impressed, and began seriously thinking and praying about whether or not he should join the church.

He decided to go out into the desert to fast and pray. There, he had an unusual experience. After fasting and praying for most of the day, he had a vision. He did not understand its meaning. He wanted to tell us the vision and see if we knew what it meant. We told him we would be happy to hear the vision and try to help him understand its meaning if we could.

In his vision, he was in a large room filled with thousands of people. At the front of the room, a holy person stood behind an altar. Beyond the altar was a veil. Occasionally, people would get up and go to the front of the room, where the person standing behind the altar would help them to pass through the veil. Brother Benjamin observed that I was in the vision. I had never had a vision and was surprised that an investigator had a vision and that I was in it. In his vision, I was kneeling, blindfolded, in front of the altar while people from the congregation came up to go through the veil. An angelic person took Brother Benjamin by the hand and led him toward the altar. Then the vision ended.

He asked if we knew what the vision meant. I asked him, "When you were in the vision, do you know which direction you were facing?" He thought about it for a minute. "I was facing East." That confirmed my impression that the setting was like a room in the Salt Lake Temple. The meaning of the vision immediately came to my mind. I told him that the Holy Ghost had revealed to me that all the people in the room were those to whom I would teach the gospel throughout my life. Those who got up from the congregation, went to the front, and passed through the veil were those who received the things that were taught. The blindfold was symbolic of my not knowing who would respond to the gospel message. I explained to Brother Benjamin that he was one of those people, and whether or not he was able to pass through the veil into the presence of the Lord depended on how he responded to the principles and teachings of the gospel that my companion and I were teaching him.

I told him that he was going to have to exercise his own faith and his own obedience and decide whether or not he would respond to the teachings of the gospel and continue progressing until he was able to re-enter the presence of the Lord. Otherwise, he could choose to stay with the many people who heard the teachings but never progressed to go through the veil.

He was very inspired by the vision and interpretation but he was not sure if he had enough knowledge and faith to be able to move ahead. We continued to meet with him. He didn't immediately decide to get baptized and move ahead like we hoped he would. It was a difficult decision for him because of his background. He was struggling with it, but seemed to be slowly moving toward baptism.

Then I was transferred and lost contact with Brother Benjamin. I don't know if he was baptized or not. I have often thought of him and hoped that he was. I have reflected many times on his vision, and my role in it. I eventually became a seminary and institute teacher, and have taught many other classes in the church. I feel that Brother Benjamin's vision helped reveal part of my life mission: I would be blessed with the opportunity to teach thousands of people and to help them to progress closer to the Lord, but I would not often know the final outcome of my teaching.

Study Questions

1. If you have ever tried to "counsel your God" what was the result?

2. Why do some people receive visions while others do not? (See Ether 12:6)

3. Is there a way that you can relate the vision described in this chapter to your life?

CHAPTER 2
Seagulls and Crickets

"For behold the field is white already to harvest…" (D&C 4:4)

When I was serving as a missionary in Glendale, California, my companion and I prayed one morning about what the Lord would have us do that day. We were going to go out tracting and we earnestly prayed for directions to where we should knock on doors and contact people. We looked at the map of our area and considered it very carefully. We had a feeling that we should go to one particular area, so we got in the car and started driving there. On the way, we noticed a young woman walking on the side of the road. She was carrying what looked like a bag of groceries, and she had an obvious limp. After we passed her, I turned to my companion. "I think we should talk to that woman." We turned around and went back to where she was, but by then she had turned into a side street. It was a cul-de-sac with only about ten houses on it. The young woman with the groceries and the limp was nowhere in sight.

We were baffled that we had lost her so quickly, but decided that we would just knock on all the doors in the cul-de-sac to find her. When we knocked at the second house on the right, a woman answered the door, but she was not our mystery woman. We introduced ourselves.

She smiled. "Oh, I've been waiting for you! My name is Joan."

I was confused. "You've been waiting for us? How long?"

She exclaimed, "Years!"

"Great! We'd like to meet with you and your family to teach you about Jesus Christ and his restored church."

"Okay, good deal."

We made an appointment to return in a few days. When we went back to teach Joan, she and her son listened intently. Her husband wasn't interested in receiving the discussions, but also was not available because he had to work nights. The discussions with Joan and her son were wonderful. She was very intelligent, funny, and receptive. There were many spiritual experiences, and there was much laughter. She had a master's degree and taught history at a local high school. We went through several discussions pretty rapidly and things were progressing extremely well with no serious issues.

One time, after we had gone through several lessons, I just had to ask, "You know, this all seems to be going so smoothly. It seems to be so easy for you to believe and accept everything we're teaching you. Why is that?"

She shrugged. "Well, the seagulls ate the crickets, didn't they?"

I didn't understand. "What?"

She explained, "You know when the pioneers came to the Salt Lake Valley? The seagulls ate the crickets, didn't they?"

I was surprised. "Well, yes they did."

She continued, "It's a well-documented fact that it actually happened. I read about it in history years ago. When I read that, I figured the Mormon church must be true and I've just been waiting for someone to come along and tell me about it."

We thought that was wonderful. We continued to teach Joan and her son the rest of the lessons and it wasn't long before they were baptized. In one of our last discussions before she was baptized, she announced, "I had a sort of dream or vision that I'd like to tell you about."

My companion and I were curious. "Wonderful! Please tell us about it."

"Elder Van Shaar, you were in it. I was asking the Lord to show me what was going to happen in the last days. There were a large number of people who had to leave California and go to Utah because of riots and other problems. I didn't know where to go or what to do, so I prayed and asked for guidance. Then I saw your face and recognized you, and that was the end of my vision."

She asked me if I knew what it all meant. I thought about it for a minute. "Well, there is a pretty good chance that some time in the last days, people might have to leave some places and go to others, including going to Utah. I don't know why you would see my face. Maybe because I taught you the gospel or maybe I'll have something to do with helping you get to where you need to be." It was kind of a simple vision, but I've thought about it many times during the last 45 years. She would be very old now and the Saints in California still haven't had to flee to Utah.

Shortly after her baptism, I was transferred to another area, so I don't know what happened to her after that, but I do know that she was a wonderful person. It was a highlight of my mission to work with her and her son. Many years later, after I related this story to my daughter, she asked, "What about the lady with the limp?" I told her that we tracted out the rest of the street and most of the people weren't home. The few who were home weren't interested. We asked Joan about the lady with the limp, but she had no idea who it might have been. She didn't know of anybody matching that description who lived on her street. So, we never did find the lady with the limp, but she led us to Joan.

Discussion Questions

1. When you are trying to get inspiration about what to do, why is it usually important to actually start doing something?

2. Why is it important to ask people how they feel and what they think?

3. Why do people often overlook or ignore obvious things like the seagulls and crickets?

4. Why do investigators or students sometimes have spiritual experiences that the teacher has not?

CHAPTER 3

Deceptive Spirits

"And it came to pass, as we went to prayer, a certain damsel possessed with a spirit of divination met us." (Acts 16:16)

During the first year of my mission, I was transferred to a city in southern California. Soon afterward, my companion and I went to the home of some newly baptized members for a dinner appointment. Frank and Hannah were a young couple with two small children. They were very friendly, seemed happy, and the meal was delicious. After the meal we had a pleasant discussion. Hannah mentioned several things that the Spirit had told her. At first, I assumed that she was a very spiritual person talking about what might be described as "typical inspiration."

So that you may better understand what happened next, let me tell you what had happened previous to this dinner appointment, unbeknownst to me. When the missionaries first went to their door, Hannah was very receptive and consented to have them return and teach her and her husband a missionary discussion. The first discussion went so well that it was only a few weeks until they had received most of the missionary discussions and were preparing for baptism. Frank and Hannah had by then both expressed that they had felt the Holy Spirit testify to them and that they believed in the restored gospel of

Jesus Christ. Hannah explained to the missionaries that during the last year, she often communicated with the Spirit by writing down questions and letting the Spirit write the answers. The missionaries thought and prayed about this and decided that it was not from the Holy Spirit. They went to her home to advise her to stop that procedure. When she opened the door, she was very excited and told them that she had asked the spirit in writing if she should get baptized. The spirit had told her yes. She said that she and Frank wanted to be baptized as soon as possible. The missionaries decided to proceed with the baptism and not deal with the spirit writing issue.

Now, back to our conversation at the dinner appointment. I asked Hannah about some of her spiritual experiences and she explained her "spirit writing" procedure. I immediately knew that something was wrong. As soon as I started to respond to her, I felt the influence and guidance of the Holy Spirit in a miraculous way. It felt like he was giving me the words to say, and yet at the same time I realized that I had previously learned but forgotten most of what I was saying. I spoke without interruption for about a half an hour, marvelling all the while at what was transpiring. One of the things I did was to read Acts:16:16-18 which says, "And it came to pass, as we went to prayer, a certain damsel possessed with a spirit of divination met us, which brought her masters much gain by soothsaying: The same followed Paul and us, and cried, saying, These men are the servants of the most high God, which shew unto us the way of salvation. And this did she many days. But Paul, being grieved, turned and said to the spirit, I command thee in the name of Jesus Christ to come out of her. And he came out the same hour." I explained that even though the woman was telling the truth she was still being influenced by a deceptive spirit, which Paul detected and cast out.

The Holy Spirit then prompted me to repeat some things I had previously read from *The Teachings of the Prophet Joseph Smith*. I explained to Frank and Hannah that she was being influenced by a deceptive spirit, even though it had sometimes told her the truth, and that she needed to refrain from all spiritual interactions which do not conform to the scriptures and teachings of the prophets. All of us felt the power of the Holy Ghost testifying so strongly that we all were convinced of the truth of everything that had been spoken. Hannah committed to abide by what had been taught. We informed her that if necessary, we could help her by the power of Christ's priesthood, even as Paul did. We also told them that they could call us anytime if they needed help.

A few days later, we received a phone call in the middle of the night from Frank. He told us that Hannah had refused to communicate with the spirit and as a result they had heard, seen, and felt some terrifying things. He was very upset and asked if we could quickly come and help. We said we would get there as soon as we could. We dressed hastily and drove to their house. On the way there, things seemed normal until we turned onto their street. We were suddenly filled with fear and dread, and when we pulled up in front of their house, we were afraid to get out of the car. My companion and I felt duty-bound to proceed to the house, even though we were being pummeled by fear. When we got to the door, we were afraid to knock, but we did so anyway because of the love we felt for these people. Frank was wide-eyed and trembling when he opened the door. An oppressive spirit immediately engulfed us so that we could hardly speak, walk, or even stand upright. We struggled to enter the home, but as soon as we did, we quickly knelt and I raised my right arm to the square. "In the name of Jesus Christ and by the power of the Melchizedek Priesthood we command you to depart."

The fear and dread instantly left the room. Peace and light were everywhere. We all felt wonderful. In the next few weeks, we repeated this process several times. Eventually, these problems ceased and Frank and Hannah went on to become very solid in the church. Hannah continued to be extremely receptive to the Holy Spirit and his inspiration. Through this and subsequent experiences, I learned that it is possible for good people, who are spiritually sensitive, to receive revelation from both the light and the dark side.

Many years later when I was teaching institute in New Mexico, a student told me that she was troubled by two spirits. She was single, about 28 years old, and was quite unhappy. She told me that she had regular communication with the spirits, and that they were very profane. I told her that for her own good she needed to avoid any such communications. I also told her that if she needed help with this issue, she should request a priesthood blessing. She asked me if I would be willing to give her a blessing. I told her it would be best to have her bishop do it, but I would be willing to help if needed. The next time she talked with me, she reported that she told the two spirits that I might come and cast them out. They told her that they knew me well and hated me. I was stunned by that information and immediately began to fast and pray in order to be prepared to cast them away. However, she soon made some changes in her life and told me that they had ceased to trouble her.

While I was teaching institute in Missouri, a student came to my office to see me. At the time, I was both her institute teacher and bishop. We had some good interviews in which she confessed numerous things. She told me that she had made many sacrifices to change her life around and get on the right track. She had even moved to that area in order to escape some very negative influences. However, she was still very troubled and asked for a priesthood blessing. As I gave her the blessing, I suddenly felt a prompting to cast out an evil spirit, which I did as part of the blessing. I was surprised by what had happened and wanted to discuss it with her, but she left quickly. Less than an hour later, she returned and wanted to talk. She explained to me that prior to the blessing, she felt like everything she saw and heard seemed to be hazy, and following the blessing, everything was perfectly clear. The last I heard about her, she was happily married in the temple and had a family.

A few years later, I was a home teacher to a single parent family consisting of a mother and two sons. This family had lots of problems and lived in an old dilapidated mobile home that was right next to the grandmother's house. One day the grandmother called me and told me that one of the grandsons was possessed by an evil spirit and that she wanted me to come and cast it out. I told her that I would get back to her. I called the bishop, explained the situation, and asked how he wanted to handle it. He told me that he would take care of it. Later, he told me that he had gone and picked up the boy. He took him home, chopped some wood together, fed him dinner, and had a good talk. He also told me that he thought the boy was fine but he thought the grandma had some issues and was imagining things.

Lesson Insights:

I included this last incident because I feel that it is crucial to not be preoccupied with, or jump to conclusions about misleading spirits. Most people I know haven't had, and may never have obvious experiences with deceptive spirits. That is a good thing because such experiences should be avoided if possible since they can be fearsome and destructive.

The parts of the book that I summarized for Frank and Hannah from *The Teachings of the Prophet Joseph Smith* are as follows:

> One great evil is, that men are ignorant of the nature of spirits; their power, laws, government, intelligence, etc., and imagine that when there is anything like power, revelation, or vision manifested, that it must be of God... The Shaker will whirl around on his heel, impelled by a supernatural agency or spirit, and think that he is governed by the Spirit of God; and the Jumper will jump and enter into all kinds of extravagances... Is God the author of all this? If not of all of it, which does He recognize? Surely, such a heterogeneous mass of confusion never can enter into the kingdom of heaven... A man must have the discerning of spirits before he can drag into daylight this hellish influence and unfold it unto the world in all its soul-destroying, diabolical, and horrid colors; for nothing is a greater injury to the children of men than to be under the influence of a false spirit when they think they have the Spirit of God. Thousands have felt the influence of its terrible power and baneful effects. Long pilgrimages have been undertaken, penances endured, and pain, misery and ruin have followed in their train; nations have been convulsed, kingdoms overthrown, provinces laid waste, and blood, carnage and desolation are habiliments in which it has been clothed... The world always mistook false prophets for true ones, and those that were sent of God, they considered to be false prophets, and hence they killed, stoned, punished and imprisoned the true prophets... whilst they cherished, honored and supported knaves, vagabonds, hypocrites, impostors, and the basest of men... The Apostles in ancient times held the keys of this Priesthood—of the mysteries of the Kingdom of God, and consequently were enabled to unlock and unravel all things

pertaining to the government of the Church, the welfare of society, the future destiny of men, and the agency, power and influence of spirits; for they could control them at pleasure, bid them depart in the name of Jesus, and detect their mischievous and mysterious operations when trying to palm themselves upon the Church in a religious garb, and militate against the interest of the Church and spread of truth. We read that they 'cast out devils in the name of Jesus,' and when a woman possessing the spirit of divination, cried before Paul and Silas, 'these are the servants of the Most High God that show unto us the way of salvation,' they detected the spirit. And although she spake favorably of them, Paul commanded the spirit to come out of her, and saved themselves from the opprobrium that might have been heaped upon their heads, through an alliance with her, in the development of her wicked principles, which they certainly would have been charged with, if they had not rebuked the evil spirit. (*TPJS*, 203-207)

It is vital to remember that the works of darkness are most often accomplished in the ways warned about in the following scripture:

For behold, at that day shall he rage in the hearts of the children of men, and stir them up to anger against that which is good. And others will he pacify, and lull them away into carnal security, that they will say: All is well in Zion; yea, Zion prospereth, all is well—and thus the devil cheateth their souls, and leadeth them away carefully down to hell. And behold, others he flattereth away, and telleth them there is no hell; and he saith unto them: I am no devil, for there is none—and thus he whispereth in their ears, until he grasps them with his awful chains, from whence there is no deliverance." (2 Nephi 28:20-22)

Study Questions

1. What are some of the ways we can tell the difference between the Spirit of the Lord and deception? (Galatians 5:22-23; D&C 46:8-9, 27)

2. Why does it sometimes require courage to teach the truth?

3. Can you explain in your own words the main ideas Joseph Smith taught in the long quote above?

CHAPTER 4
This Could Save Your Life

"Verily I say unto thee, Thou shalt by no means come out thence, till thou hast paid the uttermost farthing." (Matthew 5:26)

The Sermon on the Mount is more than some nice things Jesus said. It contains commandments that he wants us to know and keep. "Whosoever therefore shall break one of the least of these commandments, and shall teach men so, he shall be called the least in the kingdom of heaven: but whosoever shall do and teach them, the same shall be called great in the kingdom of heaven." (Matthew 5:19)

I've often asked institute students to read Matthew 5, 6 and 7 and come to class with an insight from those chapters that's been important in their life, or an experience that's related to something in those chapters. We have had many wonderful lessons using that approach. You may want to take a break and go read those chapters now. I'll share a few verses here.

Agree with thine adversary quickly, whilst thou art in the way with him; lest at any time the adversary deliver thee to the judge, and the judge deliver thee to the officer, and thou be cast into prison. Verily I say unto thee, Thou shalt by no means come out thence, till thou hast paid the uttermost farthing. (Matthew 5:25, 26)

When I first came across that as a seminary student, I didn't understand how it applied to me. I did not understand about "agreeing with your adversary" or paying "the uttermost farthing." I also struggled with these similar verses:

> Ye have heard that it hath been said, An eye for an eye, and a tooth for a tooth: [which is referring to the law of Moses] But I say unto you, That ye resist not evil: but whosoever shall smite thee on the right cheek, turn to him the other also. And if any man will sue thee at the law, and take away thy coat, let him have thy cloak also. And whosoever shall compel thee to go a mile, go with him twain. Give to him that asketh thee, and from him that would borrow of thee, turn thou not away. Ye have heard that it hath been said, Thou shalt love thy neighbor, and hate thine enemy. But I say unto you, love your enemies, bless them that curse you, do good to them that hate you, and pray for them which despitefully use you and persecute you; That you may be the children of your Father which is in Heaven: for he maketh his sun to rise on the evil and on the good, and he sendeth rain on the just and on the unjust. For if ye love them which love you, what reward have ye? do not even the publicans the same? And if you salute your brethren only, what do ye more than others? do not even the publicans the same? And if ye salute your brethren only, what do ye more than others? do not even the publicans so? Be ye therefore perfect, even as your Father which is in heaven is perfect. (Matthew 5:38-48)

When we hear Matthew 5:48, "Be ye therefore perfect," we do not often remember that it is in the context of loving your enemies. An important part of becoming perfected is learning to love not just our friends, but also our enemies. I always had a hard time understanding about loving my enemies. I learned when I was in grade school and in junior high that if you let people pick on you, they keep picking on you. Sometimes, I had to stand up to bullies and fight back.

Jesus was not telling us that criminals should not be punished according to the law. There are many places in the scriptures and teachings of the prophets where we are taught that it's important that there be laws and punishments associated with those laws. He was not telling us that we should not exercise the right of self-defense. We are taught that the Lord expects us to defend ourselves. However, instead of talking more about what Jesus did not mean, I would like to discuss what he did mean, and how to apply it.

When I was a senior in college, my wife and I had one child and another on the way. We lived in Ogden, Utah at the time, and I was going to Weber State College. I didn't have any scholarships or grants, and it was difficult to make ends meet. I had to get jobs where I could work many hours and make a good hourly wage in order to make enough money to get by.

One of those jobs was working at a turkey processing plant in a rough part of town. I was hired to be the foreman of the clean-up crew. I was responsible for 16 crew members. Our job was to clean up the entire plant so that it would be ready to start processing the next day. Generally, we would work from about 5:00 p.m. until midnight, or until the plant was clean. We used all kinds of cleaning implements: steam hoses, high pressure soap guns, hot water hoses, scrubbing brushes, and chemicals. We usually worked 7 to 8 hours. It was a difficult and dirty job.

I'll tell you a little bit about the turkey plant process because it is an important part of the setting of this story. It also gives insight into the working conditions inside the plant. In the turkey plant, they had an area where the turkeys came in, called the killing room. They took live turkeys off the delivery trucks and hung them by their feet in brackets that moved on long conveyor-chains that carried the turkeys upside-down around the room. The turkeys fought and flapped, flinging feathers and dust in the air and all over the floor and walls.

A worker waited on a rubber mat for the turkeys to come to him. He wore an electric ring over a big rubber glove in his left hand. He grabbed the turkeys by the neck and shocked them to make them go stiff. Then he cut their necks with the knife he held in his right hand, killing one after another, thousands a day.

The turkeys then went into an area called the blood tunnel. It's important that the blood be drained from the meat, and that occurred as they continued on the conveyor through the blood tunnel. Next, the conveyor chain took them up into the feather room. The feather room had whirly-things with rubber fingers on them that beat the feathers off the turkey. They didn't bruise because the blood was gone by then.

Then, the conveyor carried the featherless turkeys over a big, long, stainless steel trough that went down through a long room. Workers stood on the side of the trough and cut open the turkeys and took out the insides, which were dropped in the trough. Water ran in the trough and washed the innards down to a conveyor belt with cups that caught the guts and carried them up and dropped them into large metal bins. They were hauled away to be used by feed companies. A lot of the innards fell off of the conveyor into an area known as the gut pit. After that, the process was a lot less disgusting. The turkeys went into large long chillers flowing with water and ice. Then they went into the boning room where they were cut up and packaged as frozen whole turkeys or turkey pieces.

At the end of each day, there was a lot of grease, blood, guts, and feathers and other filth to clean up. There were some cleanup jobs that were so dirty that crew members refused to do them. If I told them they had to do a certain dirty job or be fired, they would just walk. Therefore, the really, really, dirty, hard stuff, I had to do myself. Sometimes I had to lay down in coagulated blood with just my face up above bloody water to clean out drains. Sometimes I was over my head in turkey guts in the gut pit, with my eyes closed and my fingers holding my nose, cleaning out drains. But I've always had a strong stomach. I could tell many stories about gross things that happened there. (I could also tell you about some worse things at my next job, helping with dead bodies at the mortuary.)

Luckily, with that kind of equipment, water fights can be awesome, so it wasn't completely awful. But we did have to work hard to get the entire plant ready for work to start again in the morning. If everything was not cleaned spotless, the plant could not open the next day, and if it could not open, I would lose my job. If I lost my job I would not be able to provide for my family and go to college.

I had to be back at the plant at six in the morning to go on a full plant inspection with the USDA inspector. We called him "The Doctor." He literally put on white gloves and inspected everything in the plant. He reached under and behind anything he could, and if he found the least little bit of grease or dirt, he insisted that it be cleaned before we could start operation that day. I went with him while he looked for areas that we had missed.

The reality was that he always had to find something wrong to prove that he was doing his job. I learned very quickly that I needed to leave a little something that was obvious for him to find, that was easy to clean up, so that he could find it and write it up. Then we could clean it up in time to start the plant at 8:00. They hired people to come in early from the day crew to be there to help clean up in case we needed them, so that the plant could start running. Hundreds of employees and hundreds of thousands of dollars worth of equipment needed to start at 8:00. Every few minutes of delay cost a huge amount of money. As we did the rounds, he usually found whatever I had purposely left. Many times it was something I could just do myself quickly, but sometimes we would ask the people who were there early for that specific reason to clean it up.

But one morning, the doctor didn't notice the place that I had left for him to find. He got to the end of his inspection, back at the far end of the plant in the killing room. I was concerned because I didn't want to spend any more time in the killing room than I had to. The people who worked in there were an unsavory bunch. He went in and looked around. "Okay, well, you know, there's some tarnish on some of these racks where you hang the turkeys. I want you to get some steel wool and clean the tarnish off."

No problem. I whipped some steel wool out of my pocket and got right over there and cleaned up that little bit of tarnish. He said, "Yeah, that's good. Now do them all." Well, there were hundreds of them.

I knew I was in trouble. "How about if we get them tonight?"

"No, we aren't going to start until every one of these has been scrubbed."

There were about eight guys sitting there, smoking cigarettes and drinking coffee, getting paid for doing nothing, like they did every morning. There was never anything that had to be cleaned up in their area because my crew did a good job. Also, the stuff that he was asking us to do was picky little stuff that we shouldn't have had to do anyway.

The plant manager and The Doctor were standing there beside me. I turned to those eight guys. "OK guys, sorry, but this time you're going to have to help. Most days you are here, you get paid for not doing anything, but today's going to be the exception. Everybody grab some steel wool and some scrubbing pads and solvent, and let's just quickly go through these. If we hurry we can get this done by starting time."

Those eight guys that were sitting there were not my crew. They were the day time killing room crew. They were scary people. Generally speaking, regular folks don't work in the killing room. People in the killing room quit every day. They hired new people every day. You had to wear a breathing mask when you were in there, and it was hot. There was blood and filth flying all over. The people that worked in there were really rough, scary people.

I said as positively as I could that we needed to get to work so we could get done by 8:00. The killing room crew started to cuss, swear, complain and gripe. I figured that was par for the course and we'd just deal with it. I stayed there and encouraged them to get working. The Doctor and the plant manager left, and I was the only supervisor there. Some of the crew got a few cleaning things and walked over to start cleaning the racks. One guy, Rick, however, walked up and got right in my face and started screaming at me. He swore and yelled at me in the rudest, most profane, most violent way that I had ever experienced in my life.

He said that if my crew and I had done our job then there would not be a problem, that it was all my fault, and that he was not going to do any cleaning. I continued speaking respectfully to him and encouraged him to go along. He swore at me more, saying how horrible I was, and then he started in on my mother. I cannot convey to you how profane and violent his words were. He continued screaming. I was thinking, "This guy is out of control, what am I going to do?"

I needed to get the cleaning done, but those guys weren't working. Rick was waging a serious personal attack against me. Then he told me what he was going to do to me, how he was going to beat me up, knock my teeth out, mash in my face, and so on. He was very, very agitated. Eventually, something inside of me kind of snapped. "Okay, go for it."

He was shocked. "What?"

I answered, "If you're so tough and you're going to do all that stuff to me, go ahead. Give it your best shot."

I wasn't a great fighter, but I had been in a few fights, had played football and had even taken a few karate classes. I just figured that I was not going to stand there and take any more, and I would fight the guy if I had to. He started to swing at me and then he stopped and turned around and started pounding on the wall, really hard. I thought that was weird. Why did he say all this stuff to me and then start pounding on the wall? While he was screaming and hitting the wall, I just turned around and walked off. I came back a few minutes later and was surprised to see all the killing crew scrubbing the racks. About a half hour later I came back with The Doctor. He looked at the racks and decided it was good enough. The plant started production on time. I left and drove across town to go to class and be a normal college student and didn't think anything more about it.

That night, work went pretty much as usual until about midnight. That's when I realized that I had forgotten to put in the trucks. In back of the plant, there was an alley with an old street lamp next to an area enclosed by an eight foot high fence with razor wire around the top. Every night the trucks needed to be parked in that enclosure with the gate locked. Making sure that the trucks were pulled in and the gate was locked was part of my job. I usually did it right after I got there, before it was dark. But that particular night, I forgot. I remembered about midnight and went to take care of the trucks.

I walked through the plant and past a cleaning crew member who was in the killing room. I told him that I was heading out to do the trucks and I'd be back in a minute. I opened the big metal door and started to walk out. I saw movement out there and wondered what I should do. I could have gone back and got some of the guys to go out with me. I could have called the police, but what would I say? I thought whatever happened, I could handle it. I threw open the door and ran out, went across the way, jumped in a truck, started it up and pulled it in the gate. I did that with all four trucks, closed the gate and locked it, and was relieved that it was done.

Then I turned around and started to walk across the alley toward the back of the plant. At that moment, a guy came out of the shadows. He walked up and stood right in front of me. It was Rick, the guy from the killing room crew who had accosted me that morning. He was standing right there between me and the door. He just stood there and didn't say anything for a while. I stood there and didn't say anything either. Then other guys started coming out of the shadows. There were about ten of them. They came out and stood in a big circle around me. I just stood there.

Rick smirked. "You remember me?"

I didn't say anything.

"This morning you said you were ready to fight so I'm here to take care of that now."

I still didn't say anything. I didn't know what to say or what to do. He said he was going to beat me up like he had threatened that morning. He suddenly swung his fist. I wasn't really ready for it. He hit me on the jaw. My glasses and my plastic helmet flew off and bounced on the ground. He hit me pretty hard, but it didn't knock me down.

You may not know this, but sometimes if you are playing football or something rough, and you get hit, it can knock you out or hurt you, but sometimes it just wakes you up. It's like,

"Oh, that's what we're doing here, I'm ready now." That's what happened then. I was instantly more alert and ready to fight to defend myself. I bent down a little. He aimed his foot at my crotch. I was ready and caught his ankle with crossed hands and lifted it high in the air as I lunged forward.

That caught him by surprise and put him off-balance with his foot in the air. I pushed up and forward with my whole strength, which lifted him right up off the ground and carried him backward a few feet. He landed hard on his back. When he hit the ground, it knocked his breath out. All the other guys moved toward me and I stepped back. He was lying there heaving, trying to catch his breath. The other guys looked at him, and then looked at me and back at him.

After a minute, he caught his breath and got up. "Oh, you think you're a tough guy, eh?"

He took off his shirt, revealing heavy muscles, knife scars, and old bullet wounds. I did not know at the time that he was the leader of the worst criminal gang in the area. He had recently been released from the penitentiary on parole. He had been in prison for killing somebody. One of the conditions of his parole was that he get and keep a job. If he lost his job, he would be sent back to prison. That's why he didn't hit me that morning. He knew if he did, he would have lost his job and gone back to prison. I didn't know anything about that. Everybody from that area knew who he was, but I had never heard of him. He and his gang carried knives and chains and guns in their cars and the police tried to avoid dealing with them. Do you know what happens if you "dis" or disrespect a gang leader? A gang leader's life depends on him not taking any guff from anybody any time. Anybody who seriously challenges him has to be hurt or killed. That's the way it works with gangs. Without knowing it, I was in way over my head.

Rick snarled, "Before, I was just going to beat you to a pulp for disrespecting me this morning, but now I'm going to kill you slowly." Then he told me what he was going to cut off and all the horrible things he was going to do to me. He was kind of working his way around and getting ready. The other guys were laughing.

I was standing there thinking, "Oh no, I'm going to die. There's nothing in my patriarchal blessing about this. I'm married, I've got a child. What am I going to do? I'm going to get killed here!" While he was carrying on, I prayed, big time. "Lord, I need your help, I need it now! I'm going to get killed! Quick, do something." There did not seem to be an answer. I wondered, "Why is this happening to me?"

When I thought that, I heard a very clear and powerful voice in my mind that whispered, "Agree with thine adversary whiles thou art in the way with him ... and verily I say unto thee, Thou shalt by no means come out thence, till thou hast paid the uttermost farthing." (Matthew 5:25-26) I recognized that those words were from the Sermon on the Mount. It hit me hard. It seemed strange that scriptures were coming into my mind just as I was about to be killed. Suddenly I understood how it applied to my situation. I realized that if I had handled things differently that morning, it would have resulted in a very different outcome that night.

For example, if I could go back to when Rick was screaming in my face, I could very easily have responded, "Rick, I understand how you feel. You don't have to do this cleanup. Just go over there, sit down and relax. I'll take care of it for you." If I had said that, he would have gone over and sat down and had his smoke and his coffee, and he would have looked big to all the guys there. He might have been my buddy after that. He might even have defended me against others.

I knew that I had been too proud to agree with mine adversary quickly when I was in the way. Therefore, I was in a situation where I was going to have to pay the uttermost farthing. I thought, "I get it! I understand now." I know that there are times when you have to defend yourself, but most of the time in a war of words, you don't have to defend yourself. There are usually ways out of it if you will be humble, loving, kind, and agreeable. At that intense moment, it was like a big light went on. I thought, "Now I understand and I will never be the same as I was before, because now I see what Jesus was talking about." And then I thought, "Well, that's fine, but this is a little late for me to have this great spiritual insight." Rick stepped toward me, and I thought, "Okay, this is it."

Then all of a sudden, the big metal door on the back of the plant flew open and somebody came running out. The guys inside the plant had seen what was going on out back. They gathered up the whole crew to watch what was happening from the safety of the back door. Some wanted to come out to help me. Others argued against it. They knew who was out there and there was no way they were going to face them. They were having a big argument about whether or not they would come help me, and the guys who did not want to come out were winning.

The littlest guy there was a high school student named John. He was the youngest guy on the crew. He was not what you'd call a tough guy, but he was courageous. "We've got to go out and help him now!" John slammed open the door and came running out. Some of the other fifteen guys grabbed the door and pulled it shut, staying inside. That one little guy, John, came running out, yelling, "I called the cops! I called the cops!"

Rick turned to face John and demanded, "Who called the cops?" Rick moved toward John and John was running toward him. I thought, "Oh no!" Just before they came together, John turned in midair and took off running as fast as he could down the alley. His turn in midair and his run down the alley reminded me of Wile E. Coyote. John worked up in the feather room and as he went under the streetlight, I could see feathers flying off of him. He looked like he was going about 100 miles an hour down that alley with Rick chasing him. Rick was big and slow and half-drunk, and I could see there was no way he was going to catch John. Two or three of the gang took off and followed Rick.

As I stood there watching John pull away from the pursuit, I asked myself, "Why didn't you do that?" I had played halfback and fullback. I was a fast runner, faster than John. I asked myself again, "Why didn't you do that?"

That same voice in my head gave me the answer, "Because of your pride."

At that moment, something inside of me changed. I thought, "Never again will I be in a confrontation when I don't have to be. Never again will I be too proud to run."

I was standing there having my second great spiritual experience within a few minutes, when I noticed that there were still about six of those guys left around me. I looked at them, and they looked at me, and then they started closing up the circle and moving in toward me. I thought, "Oh, boy, here it comes."

Just then I heard the siren. John really had called the police before he came out. The gang heard it and I heard it. We all listened as the siren came closer. They looked at me, and I looked at them, and then they took off. They started running the direction John and Rick and the other guys went.

Just then the back door of the plant flew open and my crew ran out. The police car pulled up. I called to my crew, "We've got to go help John." I took off running and one of my crew followed me.

It wasn't very long until we caught up with the slowest gang member. He turned around. "Two-on-one, huh?" He reached in his pocket and snapped out a switchblade. I looked at my coworker and he looked at me. Then we both turned and ran as fast as we could the other way. I had learned my lesson.

When we got back around the building, there were a couple of police cars and at least four cops there. They were busy arresting my crew. My crew had their hands up on the building and on the car. I ran up to the police. "No, no! They went that way! This is my crew."

I explained that some of the gang were chasing one of our guys. I told them which way they went and that some of them had jumped in a car and sped away. The cops jumped in their cars, turned on their sirens again and tore off in that direction. I was left standing there with the rest of my crew. We went in and locked the back door and went into the lunchroom to sit and wait.

Eventually, the cops came back and took a statement from us. They didn't catch any of the gang, but they would do whatever they could. They did not know what happened to John, so we continued to wait and watch for him. About a half hour later, John walked in. He had run and run, and no one came close to catching him. Eventually, he circled around and came back.

In less than a year, I started teaching seminary full-time. One of my students happened to be a little guy named John. He was a good student, but I would have given him an "A" even if he wasn't. He had saved my life and had proved himself to be a young man of courage.

That night, Rick and his gang got away from the cops and re-grouped. They went looking for the next guy on Rick's list of enemies. They found him in a bar and killed him. They were observed and the police arrested Rick. The next day he was taken back to prison.

Everything at work was normal after that, which is why I'm still here to tell the story. I learned some things that night that I've applied many times since then. I'm not perfect at it, but I'm way better than I used to be. If you understand what Jesus taught in Matthew chapter five and if you understand the true story I just shared, it could save your life.

Men and young men, if you're walking down the street with your girlfriend or your wife, and some guy starts shouting obscenities at her, what are you going to do? You are going to look the other way and pretend you didn't hear and keep on walking. You don't know who you are dealing with, and Jesus has already told you how to handle it.

This same principle applies every single day in normal life. It applies in the family, workplace, at school, and with friends. We can do a lot to smooth our way through life by picking our battles carefully.

Discussion Questions

1. How do you think you might benefit from studying the Sermon on the Mount?

2. Why do you suppose I included so many details about the turkey plant? How could such a distasteful job or context possibly relate to your life?

3. In this chapter I told about revelations that came during a time of great distress. What applications might this have in your life?

4. What are the most important things you learned from this chapter and how will you apply them?

CHAPTER 5
Teaming up with Duke

*"You may, figuratively speaking, pound one Elder over the head
with a club, and he does not know but what you have handed him
a straw dipped in molasses to suck. There are others, if you speak a
word to them, or take up a straw and chasten them, whose hearts
are broken; they are as tender in their feelings as an infant, and will
melt like wax before the flame. You must not chasten them severely;
you must chasten according to the spirit that is in the person. Some
you may talk to all day long, and they do not know what you are
talking about. There is a great variety. Treat people as they are."*
(Discourses of Brigham, 150; Journal of Discourses, 8:364–368)

On my mission, I discovered that I not only enjoyed studying the gospel, but teaching it as well. I wanted to become a
seminary teacher. I learned that I would have to get a college
degree and receive additional Church Educational System
(CES) training. It would be difficult to get hired because there
were more applicants than openings. During my student teaching, I quickly found out that teaching seminary was much more
difficult than any other kind of teaching I had previously done.
However, it turned out well and I was one of the few applicants
who was hired that year. One very memorable student teaching
lesson I did was a student reenactment of the martyrdom of
Joseph and Hyrum Smith. The students used real guns shooting
blanks.

My first year as a paid professional teacher was 1972. I was hired to work at the Bonneville Seminary, associated with Bonneville High School which covered the South Ogden, Utah area. It was the same high school that I had graduated from six years earlier. I was scheduled to teach five classes of juniors each day. Even though the preparation and teaching was difficult, I really enjoyed it. I was having a great experience with my students, except for my fifth period class. Lessons that were well received and spiritual in the other four classes did not go well in fifth period. The main problem seemed to be a lack of reverence. It was an extremely frustrating experience.

On one occasion, a girl refused to sit in her seat, but insisted on sitting on the floor by the window. I walked over and sat down next to her on the floor. I encouraged her to sit in her seat and be involved with the class. She finally did, but that was only one of many distractions. There always seemed to be someone talking out of turn, causing a distraction, or creating some kind of problem. One day I had to leave class to take an emergency phone call. When I came back a few minutes later, a student was dancing on my desk, swinging his shirt around like a stripper. The class was clapping. I was shocked and appalled.

Nothing I tried in that class worked. On many occasions after fifth period I went in my office, closed the door, and cried. Several times I asked the seminary principal for help. He never came to observe the class, and didn't offer any counsel or give any other means of help at all. He believed that if there was a problem, it was my fault and that I would have to fix it. Since then, I've been around enough to know that most of the time, seminary principals and faculties are very helpful. There are standards and rules of behavior that are usually applied with all teachers and all classes. But then and there, I was on my own, and in fifth period, we were drowning.

One day, about halfway through the year, I was attempting to teach with the usual disturbance going on. I was trying to deal with it and continue the lesson as best I could. In the back of the room sat a young man named Duke. Up to this point, Duke had been a leader of the troublemakers. Imagine my surprise when Duke suddenly stood up: "I'm trying to listen to what Brother Van Shaar is saying right now! This is interesting and I want to hear it. He can't say it and I can't hear it because there's so much talking and goofing off. I want everyone to shut up so that he can teach and I can hear." Duke spoke so forcefully that everyone was flabbergasted. "If anybody causes a problem in here when Brother Van Shaar is trying to teach, he is going to have to deal with me."

Then he sat down. Everyone in the class, including me, was shocked and wide-eyed. I had no idea that Duke had any interest in the class, much less anything I taught. I gathered my thoughts and went ahead with the lesson. It was the first time in the whole year that it had been quiet in that class, and it was amazing. It didn't take long before I noticed that the Spirit was there. After about fifteen minutes, a big kid named Bert started goofing around. Once in a while during his antics, he would look back and smirk at Duke. Duke just stared at him, narrowed his eyes and nodded. When the bell finally rang, everybody left the building to walk across the street back to the high school. I did not know what would happen or what to think.

The next day when everyone came into class, it was very quiet. Bert walked into class a little late, sporting a black eye, swollen cheek, scrapes on his face, and a big fat lip. He looked a mess. As soon as he walked into the class, he made eye contact with Duke. Duke glared at him and Bert immediately looked down at the floor. He shuffled over to his desk and sat down. He didn't make a peep during the rest of the class. Later I found out the rest of the story. Right after leaving class the previous day, Duke caught him while crossing the road and started throwing punches. It was only a few seconds before he was badly beaten up, but not one person reported it to the school administration.

Many of the students in the class had seen what happened, and those that didn't see anything heard about it. In class that next day, the students looked at Bert then at Duke and they just sat there and listened. There was no disruption or irreverence of any kind. Duke just leaned back in his chair and smiled. And that's the way it went in fifth period for the rest of the year. Fifth period went from being my worst class to my best class. They got more and more interested and even began to participate in a positive way. They started singing in devotionals and the Spirit was with us most of the time.

It was amazing to me the way the nature of that class changed and continued that way for the rest of the year. I never did find out exactly why Duke changed and brought the class along with him. Over the years, I saw many students lead classes in the right direction in a positive way, but I never saw a change as dramatic as Duke's.

In those days, seminary teachers generally got another job during the summer. That summer, I was hired to be a counselor in the LDS Social Services Day Camp program. One of the directors for the Day Camp program in that area was another seminary teacher named Jordan. My first impression of Jordan wasn't very favorable but the more I got to know him, the better I liked him and we eventually became good friends.

The group that I was assigned to lead consisted of boys ages 12 to 14. All of them except one had very serious problems. Some of them had serious issues in school. Several of them were given a choice by the court to either attend day camp or go to jail. As their counselor, adviser, and leader, I was authorized to hire an assistant. It was going to be a full-time summer job for both my assistant and me. I knew that I had a difficult group to deal with so I contacted Duke. "Duke, we don't know each other very well but you had a positive effect in seminary this year and I would like to hire you to help me with a group of troubled boys." Duke took the job.

The Day Camp provided us with a limited budget and a van to drive. We were to take these troubled boys, be good examples to them, and teach them positive things through wholesome, fun activities. We didn't have any formal classes. Everything we did was activity based. On one day we'd take them to play ball. Another day we'd go tubing on the river, and so forth. They were a tough group of boys and we learned very quickly that if we stopped at a convenience store the boys would go in and steal anything they could: beer, cigarettes, junk food, whatever. We had to be very careful about where we went and what we did because those boys would find a way to get in trouble if given a chance.

Even though we spent most of the time trying to help them have fun and be happy, one of their favorite things to do was run away. It took a constant, vigilant effort to keep track of those boys. If they ran away and caused trouble, the Day Camp might be held responsible. So, we were instructed not to let them get away. There were several times some of them tried to run, but they never got very far before we caught them. Duke and I watched them closely and we were both very fast runners. Sometimes one of us would drive the van ahead of them while the other chased on foot. To their surprise, we always caught them.

We eventually realized that to maintain acceptable behavior we had to have some form of discipline within the group. Even though Duke and I were positive examples, treating them well and doing fun things with them wasn't quite enough. There was a pond in the area where we were that we often drove by. It was near the road, had moss in it, and was very stinky. Duke and I determined that a potential punishment for serious misbehavior in the group could be to be thrown into the "stink pond." We talked with the boys about it and they agreed that the stink pond was an acceptable punishment. They seemed to think that it would be funny because it would always be the other guy who would end up being thrown in the stink pond.

It wasn't very long after this new consequence was instituted that somebody acted up enough to necessitate a trip to the stink pond. Duke and I walked the culprit to the pond and threw him in. The pond was very stinky and yucky. Whoever went in had to wear those wet stinky clothes the rest of the day. One time I slipped in the stink pond and had to wash my clothes twice that night. It only took a few trips to the stink pond before nobody acted up enough to get thrown in anymore. I guess nowadays you'd get fired, sued, or arrested for something like that, but in those days nobody was upset by it: not the kids, the parents, nor the Day Camp leadership. In fact, we never even heard it being discussed outside of our group.

One time, we decided that we wanted to take our whole group to Lagoon amusement park. There wasn't enough money in our budget to pay for it so we had to raise our own money in order to go. In those days, soda pop bottles were made of glass, and stores would give you five cents for each empty bottle. As a group, we decided that we would collect pop bottles and turn them in to get the money we needed to go to Lagoon. The boys were very excited to go to Lagoon. Some of them had never been there but had heard wonderful things about it. We decided that we'd spend about half an hour every day collecting pop bottles so that we would have enough money by the end of the summer.

The first few times we went out to collect bottles it went well. But after a few days the boys realized it was not easy work and became less enthusiastic. One of the ways that we collected pop bottles was by going door to door down a street asking if anyone had bottles that they were willing to donate to us. We had the boys work down a street in pairs, with two boys on each side. Duke and I would sit in the van at the end of the street and watch.

We would move the van a block at a time picking up the collected bottles with each move. There were a lot of places where people had a few pop bottles and were happy to give them to the boys. But one day, they'd knocked on doors for a quite a while without having any success. Duke and I watched them work street after street, getting no bottles. We started getting concerned because we could see the boys getting discouraged. It felt like one of those times when they would run away. We expected them to take off at any moment. I turned to Duke. "I think we ought to pray about this."

He looked surprised. "Do you really think this is the kind of thing we ought to pray about?"

I nodded. "Yes, I do."

He shrugged. "Okay."

We closed our eyes. In the prayer, I asked that the boys would have success in getting pop bottles so that they could have a good experience from having worked at something and having it turn out well.

After the prayer ended, Duke didn't say much. We kept watching the boys. One of the residents came to their front door, talked to our boys and then just closed the door. The two boys glanced up the street at us and then quickly slipped out of sight.

Duke leaned forward. "Oh no, there they go! They're going to take off through that back yard and we're going to have to run around the other side of the block and try to catch them."

I took a deep breath. "Well Duke, let's just wait here a minute and see what happens." Then one of the boys came back to the front of the driveway and motioned for us to drive the van down there. When we got there, the garage door near the back of the house was open and inside the garage were hundreds of empty pop bottles. The boys were very excited and the homeowner was happy to be getting rid of the bottles. All the other boys came running up to help. In just a few minutes, all the bottles were being loaded in the back of the van.

Duke turned to me and asked, "Does stuff like that happen to you very often?"

"Stuff like what?"

"Like when you pray for something, and then your prayer is answered."

"Sometimes when I pray, the answer is 'Wait.' Sometimes the answer is 'No.' Sometimes there does not seem to be an answer. But yes, I often get answers to my prayers and sometimes an answer comes fast."

"Did you expect this thing with the bottles to happen when you prayed?"

"I had faith that something good would happen when we prayed."

"Wow! I never really knew that it could be like this."

"Well Duke, as you just saw, it can."

"I have a whole new outlook on this prayer thing and on other spiritual things. I know you talked about these things a lot in seminary, but I didn't realize how much they applied to me."

"They do apply to you and can lead to having many wonderful things happen in your life."

Another time we took the boys out to a different pond to have a picnic and maybe swim. It was big, clean, and blue. One of the boys, Roger, started acting up for what seemed like no reason. Duke spoke up. "Roger, come on, chill out, cool down, and relax. Everything's fine." But Roger kept hitting and pushing the other boys.

I was getting irritated. "Look, this is not the stink pond but we will throw you in if you keep this up."

Suddenly, Roger pulled out a big knife. He was only about 13 years old, but was very large for his age. The knife was made of stainless steel and had a long thick blade. He held it in front of him threateningly. "You can't tell me what to do! You're not going to throw me in the pond!"

Everyone was stunned. Duke and I just stood there looking at him. After a few seconds I decided to try to calm him down. "Look Roger, you don't want to do this. We don't need to have this kind of trouble." He got more agitated. He seemed to like the power the knife gave him and showing off in front of the other boys. I looked closely at the knife. Neither the blade nor the point looked very sharp. I kept talking and moved a little closer. Without warning, I kicked hard and fast, aiming at his knife hand. My foot hit his hand and wrist. The knife went flying. He started to shake his hand, crying that I had hurt him. I quickly picked up the knife and threw it far out into the pond.

I turned back to Roger. "Don't you ever, ever try anything like that again! Not with me, not with anybody!"

He was shocked by what had happened. It wasn't very long before he started telling us how sorry he was and that he wouldn't ever do anything like that again. "You don't have to throw me into the pond. I'll do it to myself." He turned around and walked out into the pond and dunked himself. He came back dripping. "I want you all to know that I'm sorry and that I'll never do anything like that ever again. I will be a better kid from now on." That was it. We did not tell anyone else about what had happened and there was no more trouble with Roger for the rest of the summer.

That summer, Duke and I became good friends. We felt like we had helped those boys a lot and hoped that we had made a lasting difference in their lives. Eventually, Duke fulfilled an honorable mission and was married in the temple. I've always been grateful for the way Duke saved my fifth period class and for the relationship we shared that summer.

Discussion Questions

1. Why is classroom reverence so important?
2. What might have caused Duke to change?
3. Why did the rest of the class change?
4. Why are disciplinary measures sometimes necessary?
5. How does the lesson Duke learned about prayer apply to you?
6. Why is it important to be a good friend?

CHAPTER 6
Her Last Breath?

"And again I speak unto you who deny the revelations of God, and say that they are done away, that there are no revelations, nor prophecies, nor gifts, nor healing... O all ye that have imagined up unto yourselves a god who can do no miracles, I would ask of you, have all these things passed... And if there were miracles wrought then, why has God ceased to be a God of miracles and yet be an unchangeable Being... And the reason why he ceaseth to do miracles among the children of men is because that they dwindle in unbelief, and depart from the right way, and know not the God in whom they should trust... And these signs shall follow them that believe—in my name shall they cast out devils... they shall lay hands on the sick and they shall recover; And whosoever shall believe in my name, doubting nothing, unto him will I confirm all my words, even unto the ends of the earth." (Mormon 9:7-8, 15, 18-20, 24-25)

In 1975, I was still teaching at the Bonneville Seminary in Ogden, Utah. Attending one of my classes was a senior named Lonnie. One day, she came to speak to me with utmost urgency. She had been regularly babysitting a six-month-old baby girl named Angela. But all was not well at the baby's home.

Lonnie told me that the mother was a completely inactive member of the church, unknown to the bishop or any members in the area. The mother had serious problems, and her husband, not the biological father, had abused Angela so brutally that she was now in critical care at McKay-Dee Hospital. It was sickening to me to imagine a full-grown man beating a six-month-old. The abuser was not a member of the church and had been arrested and then released on bail. It was a terrible situation. Angela had been severely injured. She suffered a fractured skull, then developed pneumonia in the hospital. Lonnie asked if I would go to the hospital and give Angela a blessing. I suggested it would be better to have it done by someone in the family or the bishop, but circumstances were such that there was nobody else available. She insisted that the baby was in critical condition and needed a blessing. She pleaded for me to do it quickly. I agreed.

When we got to the hospital, no one was in the room with Angela. Her small, fragile head was bandaged, and her little carrier had tipped over in the bed, forcing her into an almost face-down position. Each breath was so labored that I feared the next one might be her last. The fact that no one was there to help as she struggled for life was very upsetting. I called in the nurse for urgent help and asked about Angela's situation. The nurse explained that Angela was not expected to survive more than a few hours. The only visitors had been the mother for a short time several days prior and Lonnie.

We said a prayer, and I prepared to give Angela a blessing. But what could I say? What chance did this little girl have with a mother who didn't care and a man who had tried to kill her? Even if she made it through, she'd probably be exposed to more abuse, and if she managed to survive that, what kind of a life would she have? I felt like blessing her to pass away quickly so that she could enter into the peace of the spirit world and loving arms on the other side of the veil. I felt sadness, discouragement and anger.

As I began to seal the anointing and pronounce a blessing of a quick and peaceful passing, I found I could not do so. It didn't feel right. It didn't feel good. I felt restrained by the Spirit. Then the Holy Ghost told me exactly how to bless her. I followed his guidance and gave Angela a blessing of miraculous recovery. I blessed her that the full purposes for which she came to Earth would be accomplished. I blessed her that many good things would happen in her life.

When the blessing ended, I looked up. Lonnie's eyes were wide with surprise. Tears fell as we stood in silence, shocked by what had been said. All I could do was describe how the blessing had been inspired, going beyond my understanding. It had been what the Lord wanted.

The next step was to make sure somebody was always at Angela's side to see that she was watched over and taken good care of. I shared the story with my seminary students, and soon there was a group of volunteers. Many seminary students' hearts were touched by sitting in that room, listening to her ragged breaths as they prayed for her.

Within a few days, one of the nurses gave me great news. Instead of worsening, Angela had improved so much that she was now being transferred to Primary Children's Hospital in Salt Lake City. As neither Lonnie nor I were related to the little one, updates became scarce.

About two weeks later, a family in our church ward that took in foster children had a new baby with them at church. It was Angela! They explained that Child Protective Services had taken custody, and they, while not knowing the surrounding circumstances, had been given the opportunity to welcome her into their home. Though still frail in appearance, she was finally breathing strongly. We continued to see her at church until the family moved and we lost touch.

It was a very profound experience in my life and Lonnie's. I'm very thankful to have been able to extend a helping hand,

and I learned something very important. Sometimes, when we think we know what's best and try to do what's right, the Lord steps in with His wisdom and power to guide us to bless people in ways we cannot comprehend in the moment.

Lonnie was changed by this experience. She knew that what she witnessed was a miracle. She was shocked and surprised by how clear and obvious it was. Thereafter, she became more invested in the church and the gospel. Her attitude in seminary improved and she seemed to be happier.

Eventually, I lost track of Lonnie, but over a period of about thirty years, she contacted me sporadically. She'd call me on the phone or write a letter. Usually, we'd talk about the church and things that had happened in her life. There were some good times and some hard times, but she never forgot what she learned from the experience with Angela. It's been quite a few years since I've heard from her, but I trust things are going well.

As for Angela, I'm grateful to have shared that experience with her and to have seen the great blessing come to that wonderful little baby. Though I often wonder about her, I have faith she has had a good and happy life because that was her blessing from the Lord.

Discussion Questions

1. Why do you think child abuse happens?
2. Why is personal involvement critical in helping care for the sick?
3. How has the Lord surprised you or someone you know in a good way?
4. Why did this experience have such a profound effect on Lonnie?
5. Have you, or someone you know experienced a miraculous healing? Did it result in any significant attitude or life changes?

CHAPTER 7
The Miracle Hand

"And Moses cried unto the Lord, saying, Heal her now, O God, I beseech thee." (Numbers 12:13)

"Then saith he to the man, Stretch forth thine hand. And he stretched it forth; and it was restored whole, like as the other." (Matthew 12:13)

"For behold, I am God; and I am a God of miracles; and I will show unto the world that I am the same yesterday, today, and forever; and I work not among the children of men save it be according to their faith." (2 Nephi 27:23)

NOTE: Even though the other chapters in this book are written by me, it seemed best to describe this incident using the following account written by my wife, Barbra. She wrote it to our daughter to explain this accident and the miracle that followed.

An Injury and a Miracle

My brother Mike had a new 1974 Jeep and he was excited to take it out in the mountains for the deer hunt that year. October came and he asked Gene to go with him. As it turned out, that would be Mike's last deer hunt. He died on August 31, 1975, but that's a story to be told another time.

We lived in Clinton at that time, on a street that ended in a cul de sac. Our house was on the north side of that circle. It was late afternoon, probably about 4:00, when Mike and Dad got home. Mike was driving, and they had a deer, so they pulled up onto the lawn, stopping just a few feet from the front step, with the passenger side of the Jeep facing the front door.

I was home with the three children we had at that time. You were about eight months old. We heard them pull up out front, so all of us went out to see what they had brought home. The boys were pretty excited. They wanted to see the deer, whose head was hanging outside the Jeep. I was holding you and put you down on the grass next to me so you could crawl around a minute. You were at the stage in your locomotion where you were pulling up to stand by things and even taking a few shaky steps alone.

I turned for just a second or two to say hello to Dad and Mike as they started to tell about their day. The boys had moved farther out onto the lawn, on the other side of the Jeep from Dad, Mike and me. They were running around a bit and just having a generally good time. You took off crawling to my left, but I don't remember seeing you go. I think that subconsciously, I thought you had gone around to look at what your brothers doing. But one thing I did not have was any sense that you were in danger.

The accident that happened then was one of those things that left us saying, "But we only took our eyes off her for a few seconds." That is indeed the truth. We were not so deeply involved in conversation that we weren't aware of our surroundings. We were just chatting. I wasn't timing this, you know, but it really could not have been more than twenty or thirty seconds from the time I set you down on the grass until we heard you scream.

I ran around to the opposite side of the Jeep to where you were. I still did not have any sense that something serious was wrong. I thought that maybe you had crawled on a thorn, or at worst, perhaps a bee had stung you. I picked you up and looked at you to see if I could tell what was wrong, but you didn't quit crying. Then I saw your right hand and I screamed and started to shake. Your hand was terribly burned. Your fingers were all white and the palm and heel were white too except for a couple of very tiny areas. The whole burned area was already raising into a huge blister. I don't remember whether I went around to them or they came around to me, but immediately Dad and Mike were there.

It didn't take us long to reconstruct what had happened. I had set you down and you must not have wasted a second before you headed around the back of the Jeep. You had crawled to the other side, near the back of the rear tire and had reached out to pull yourself up on the exhaust pipe. The exhaust system was blazing hot from the day's drive and your tiny baby hand was burned instantly and terribly. (It is still a horrible incident to think about).

Mike and I ran into the house and to the bathroom to run cold water on the injury. I think that Dad rounded up the other kids and then called Doctor O. Wendell Hyde, our family doctor. You were screaming, I was sobbing uncontrollably and poor Mike was doing his best to hold us up and together as we stood there at the bathroom sink. I was full of too many thoughts: *Why had I put you down? How was it possible for you to get around there so fast? How badly was your hand really hurt? Could it be fixed? Why hadn't I had the sense to know that there was danger? How much did it hurt you? Why hadn't I stayed in the house with you and then talked to the men when they came in? How could you be so hurt when there were three intelligent adults who loved you very much standing right there within inches of you? Couldn't we make time go backwards for just five minutes?*

Please don't let this be happening!!! I felt sad, guilty, worried and helpless. I had never let one of my children be so hurt and I could not believe this had happened.

I begged Dad to give you a blessing then while Mike was there to help, but he would not. This is one point where Dad and I still differ, I guess. My feeling was that a blessing was needed immediately. This was an emergency and I felt a huge need for the Lord's help to get through it. I wanted that healing power to begin now! Dad, on the other hand felt that he wanted to be sure that he had his thoughts together and that he was spiritually prepared to give the blessing. My thought was, "Too late for that. Ready or not, it is time to give the blessing!" Keep in mind it was not a question of worthiness that kept Dad from giving the blessing then, but he just didn't feel ready to do it.

We headed for the doctor's office. He said he would meet us there. He took quite a bit of time looking at your hand. He was obviously concerned. He confirmed what we had thought, the burn was very serious. He suggested that we would have to wait and see how the healing process went but that skin grafts were a definite possibility at some time in the future. He warned about the danger of infection and about the necessity to keep your hand covered and clean. He also reassured us that you wouldn't be in much more pain now because all of the nerves had been burned too, but he mentioned that as it healed it would again become painful as the nerves reconnected. He covered your hand with a cream that he said was the newest treatment for burns, Silvadene. Then he wrapped your hand in gauze and an ace bandage clear up to your armpit. Since we didn't know how to make you not crawl around, it was necessary to bandage you up really well to keep dirt out of your burn. He sent us home and told us to bring you back in about ten days to have it checked. We were not to remove the bandage.

A day or two after the burn, Dad gave you a blessing. He blessed you that the hand would heal miraculously but that a scar would remain to always remind you of the love your Heavenly Father has for you.

About eight days after the accident, you were crawling around and the bandage came all undone. The gauze was still on it so I didn't see your injury, but I wrapped it back up and hurried to the doctor's office. He carefully removed the dressing and what I saw made me just sick. The skin that had been a huge blister covering most of your hand when he had wrapped it up was sloughing off in big pieces and your whole hand looked bloody and sickening. The doctor removed the dead skin and as I sat there holding back tears the best I could, he started talking about how good it looked!

One of the great things about having Doctor Hyde as our doctor was that he was also a member of the church and he understood about priesthood blessings. Dad and I told him about the blessing and he said, as he looked at your little hand, that as far as he was concerned, the miracle had already happened. He said that that bloody gore on your hand was all new growth! The skin was already growing back and it was quite certain even at that early time that there would be no need for skin grafts. He said that there would surely be considerable scarring and that it was quite possible that as you grew there would be some surgery needed to make cuts in the scar tissue to allow it to stretch to fit your hand. He said that it was time to leave the bandage off and let the air in to help it heal. He also said that since the skin was growing back, it would hurt you now because there would be healing of the nerves, too.

The next couple of weeks were painful for all of us because we still couldn't keep you from crawling around on your cracking, bleeding hand. Every time you hurt, we hurt. But within such a short time even the cracks and scabs were gone and your hand was healed. The scar remained as we knew it would, but there has never been any further problem with your hand, no skin grafts, no surgery. You have had full use of it, and it has never been a factor in limiting you from doing anything you have wanted to try.

I still wish it had not happened. I wish I had been more alert to the possibility of danger there on our front lawn. But this incident and the process that followed was a miracle in our family and was a wonderful example of the Lord's love and his willingness to bless his children.

—Barbra Van Shaar (1994)

I would like to explain why I delayed the blessing as described above in Barbra's account. When I first saw the injury, I knew that it was very serious and I quickly decided that I did not want to bless my daughter with just a partial or eventual healing. Our first visit with the doctor confirmed that skin grafts and a permanently crippled right hand were possibilities. I wanted to bless her with a quick, complete, and miraculous healing. But I was not sure if expecting such a miracle was an overreach. I spent about two days wrestling with that idea and preparing to draw on the powers of heaven. When I felt the faith and power and confirmation that she could be blessed with such a great miracle, I proceeded with the blessing. The Lord surprised me by not only blessing her with healing but also with a miraculous scar that grew as she grew to serve as a lifelong witness of a loving miracle that happened when she was too young to remember.

Discussion Questions

1. Can you empathize with how Barbra felt right after the injury?

2. Can you explain why it is usually necessary to receive medical attention along with spiritual blessings?
3. How do faith and being in tune with the will of the Lord relate to healing?
4. What are you doing to develop greater faith?

CHAPTER 8

Am I Ready?

"And for their sakes I sanctify myself..." *(John 17:19)*

I was in my mid-twenties. Barbra and I were married with two young children. We lived southwest of Ogden, Utah in Clinton. We got a wonderful deal on a two-bedroom, bi-level home with an unfinished basement in a nice new subdivision for $17,300. Another teacher at the Bonneville Seminary, Hal Cook, lived in the same subdivision and ward. We became good friends. We often played basketball and ping pong together, and our families enjoyed doing many things together.

One night when Hal's wife Lynn was nearly six months pregnant, Hal called me at about 2:00 a.m. He was very upset. There was a medical emergency with Lynn and the unborn baby. He said they needed my help and asked me to get to his house as quickly as I could. I threw on some clothes and went running out the back door. I could get to his house faster by just cutting through a couple of back yards and jumping a fence than I could by going out and starting the car and driving around. I was at Hal's house about three minutes after he called.

When I arrived, I heard loud crying and other sounds of distress. It was the most hectic and scary medical situation I had seen up to that point in my life. I knew instantly that the lives of Lynn and the baby were hanging in the balance.

Hal was shaking. "I need you to give my wife a blessing."

I was surprised by the request. "Why don't you bless her?"

He responded, "I'm too upset. I'm too emotional. I can't do it. I need you to do it. I need you to bless Lynn that she'll survive and that she'll be okay. And bless that the baby will be okay, and also bless that the baby won't be born now, because it's too early for her to survive." Then he quickly anointed his wife and suddenly it was time for me to seal the anointing and pronounce the blessing.

It was a difficult situation because I didn't have time to pray, contemplate, repent, or to fast beforehand. Even though I didn't have time to become spiritually prepared, when I laid my hands on her head, I felt the Spirit, and I felt inspiration. I felt the power of the priesthood. I blessed her that the bleeding would come under control, and that the blood she lost would not be fatal to her or the baby. I blessed her that she would be healed and that she would be well. I blessed the baby that that she would survive, and that she would be whole and well, without damage. I tried to bless the baby that she would not be born at that time, because that's what Hal had asked of me, but I couldn't do it. The Spirit restrained me from giving that blessing. I think Hal was disappointed about that. As soon as the blessing was over, she was rushed to the hospital. I stayed there to comfort their other child and help him get back to sleep.

Hal later told me that when they got to the hospital, things were touch and go, and that the doctors worked quickly to save Lynn and the baby. Not long after they got to the hospital, the baby was born. She was very premature and so small she would fit in one hand. Emergency measures had to be taken to keep her alive. Hal called and asked me to hurry to the hospital to help give her a name and a blessing because the doctors did not believe she would survive for long.

They had the baby in an incubator. There were glove-like things that we used to reach in and touch her in order to give the blessing. Hal chose to give the blessing himself and asked me to assist. He named the baby Amy and went on to bless her with many wonderful things, including that she would live, be undamaged, and have a happy life. We both cried, but they were tears of joy, not sorrow. In spite of what the doctors said, Hal and I knew that Amy was going to live and be OK.

Amy was in the hospital receiving neonatal care for a long time. But eventually, she was able to come home and experience normal growth and a happy life. She became a beautiful and intelligent child.

Lesson Insight

Many times I looked back on that incident and thought, "What would have happened if I hadn't been worthy to feel the spirit and give that blessing?" I carefully considered, "What if I wasn't ready? What if I hadn't been saying my prayers or reading my scriptures? What if I had committed sins that I hadn't repented of? Would those lives have been saved?" I don't know the answer to those questions. I assume the Lord would have done it some other way. But I was filled with gratitude that Lynn's and Amy's lives were saved, and that I was able to be a part of it. I made up my mind that from that time on, for the rest of my life, I was always going to try to be to be spiritually prepared to give a blessing and if necessary, help save a life on the spur of the moment.

Of course I knew I couldn't be perfect, but I knew that I could keep trying and keep repenting. I made that decision, not for my own sake, but for the sake of my wife, my family and anyone else who might need my help. Since then there have been many unexpected times when I needed to give a blessing to a family member or to someone else. I've been grateful that each of those times I was in a spiritual condition such that I could go ahead and give a blessing with access to the Spirit and the healing power of the priesthood.

Because of my imperfections, I have continued to be dependent on the Lord's mercy and forgiveness. Along with that I have often asked myself, "Am I ready? If I'm called upon, will I be able to bless with inspiration and power?" Jesus once said, "And for their sakes I sanctify myself…" (John 17:19) There have been many times when I might not have tried hard enough for myself. But ever since that 2 a.m. call I have been better than I would have been because I have tried to follow Jesus' example and sanctify myself "for their sakes."

Discussion Questions

1. What are you willing to do to be ready to exercise spiritual power quickly?
2. If you do not hold the priesthood, how do the principles discussed in this chapter apply to you?
3. How will remembering that Jesus said "for their sakes I sanctify myself" help you?

CHAPTER 9
Survival Hikes

"Know ye not that they which run in a race run all, but one receiveth the prize? So run, that ye may obtain. And every man that striveth for the mastery is temperate in all things. Now they do it to obtain a corruptible crown; but we an incorruptible. I therefore so run, not as uncertainly; so fight I, not as one that beateth the air: But I keep under my body, and bring it into subjection: lest that by any means, when I have preached to others, I myself should be a castaway." (1 Corinthians 9:24-27)

Over the course of a number of years, I had the opportunity to go on and lead various survival hikes. You know beforehand, of course, that a survival hike is going to stretch the limits of your physical endurance and teach you about surviving without the usual comforts. What I did not expect, however, is all the other lessons that these hikes would teach.

My first experience with a survival hike took place at the end of the summer of 1973. It was sponsored by a group associated with Brigham Young University. BYU became quite famous for their survival programs, and some commercial survival programs were spinoffs of the BYU program. At that time, I worked for LDS Social Services, supervising a group of very difficult boys. They were required to go on a survival hike as part of their summer program day camp experience. As their leader, it was part of my job to go and help supervise them on the survival hike. I felt bad that my assistant counselor, Duke, was unable to go. I would have liked to have him there.

There was a group of about forty day camp kids and leaders. We drove south from Ogden, Utah, many hours to the remote town of Escalante. Then we went further south on the dirt road that goes to the Hole in the Rock pioneer area. Before getting to Hole in the Rock, we stopped in the desert and headed off in an easterly direction toward Coyote Canyon.

We were given minimal food and the hike was designed so that we didn't have enough time to find and use survival food in the desert. We carried cracked wheat, rice, raisins, flour, honey, brown sugar, and salt to sustain us through a trek that would take longer than a week to complete. We did not have sleeping bags or camping gear. They had us bring a blanket and they gave us some straps, our basic food and some tin cans. We each had a small canteen. It was a major problem just to get your stuff tied up in the blanket with the straps and make it into a pack. Often it would fall apart as you hiked. All the kids and all the adults were expected to tie up their own makeshift packs and get them tight enough that they would not fall apart.

With these few basic supplies we started out across the desert, following the BYU survival experts. It wasn't very long until the water ran out. We all drank what water we had and we didn't come to any more water that day. That first night was called a "dry camp," which meant we had to go part of the afternoon and all night without water. I was so thirsty, and my mouth was so dry that I could hardly stand it. It was horrible. I had heard that you can get a little bit of water out of prickly pear cactus, so I tried to use my pocket knife to get the spines off so I could cut and suck it. I got a lot of pokes in my fingers and not enough liquid to make it worth the effort. Also, the cactus had a nasty taste. The only option was to suffer with thirst all night. We were too tired and thirsty to eat much that night and there was no breakfast.

The next day we got up, packed and hiked about two hours before we made it into Coyote Canyon, where water seeps, drips, and runs in very small, mossy streams on the canyon walls. With a little patience it was possible to get all we wanted to drink. After drinking and filling our canteens, we hiked without eating until mid-afternoon and camped near more seeps. During the first day and a half we hiked many miles. We did not have any meals. We ate only a few raisins, a few pinches of brown sugar, and a small amount of honey.

The second day we hiked until we made it to another place where there was water. Except for the BYU experts, none of us knew where we were going or what would happen next. That second evening they divided us up into cook groups of four. Each group had a large #10 can and each individual had an empty pop can. We were told to use matches to make a fire and cook rice for everyone in the big can. We were not told how to do it or who was to do what. All the leaders were put in separate groups from the boys and were instructed not to help the boys. We had no utensils and had to carve wooden spoons to eat with.

As soon as we were given the go-ahead, the leaders quickly worked together to gather water and firewood, light the fire, cook the rice, and eat. About two-thirds of the boys managed to work together and prepare their food. The other third (three groups) argued about who was to do what and waited for someone else to do the work, which nobody did. The BYU experts instructed the leaders to watch and wait, because an important part of this experience included giving the boys the opportunity to learn to take care of themselves. The result was that the boys in three of the groups did not have a meal that night.

The next day when we got up we were told there would be no breakfast. We started hiking. It was not long before those who had not cooperated or worked enough to eat the night before were sick and hurting. Some of them had the dry heaves and some were so weak they had difficulty hiking. It was August and very hot and we had a long way to go to the next water.

We didn't stop for lunch that day. When we finally stopped to camp at some water seeps, we were told to stay in the same cook groups and boil cracked wheat for our meal, with no additional help or instructions. It was amazing. Every cook group worked efficiently together. Nobody argued. Everyone was anxious to do whatever it took to get the food ready and eat. It continued that way for every meal for the rest of the trip.

The remainder of the hike continued in the same way. We hiked about fifty miles in all. One or two meals a day. Water shortages. Days too hot and nights too cold. Lots of strenuous hiking. The hiking eventually involved difficult climbs. We learned how to walk flat-footed on steeply slanted rock without slipping. One time we climbed a steep area using notches that were made by ancient Indians. One day we had to carefully work our way around quicksand.

There was one very difficult boy to work with in my day camp group. I will call him Darrell. He intentionally tied his pack so it would fall apart and refused to walk fast enough to keep up with the group. The BYU leaders told me that he was my responsibility and that I would have to deal with it. They were going to keep moving at the regular rate and I was to make sure that Darrell and I did not fall far enough behind that we got lost. Then they just hiked off with the rest of the group. He and I were left behind as I was working with him, trying to get his pack tied up so it would hold together. He just sat there and refused to do anything. I ended up having to tie the pack for him. By then the group was way out in front of us and I was worried about losing sight of them.

He would not walk fast enough to catch up. It happened to be one of those days when there was very little water. He and I both ran out of water and got very thirsty. We were on the verge of losing the group and getting lost. It was difficult for me to keep moving and take care of myself. The additional burden of helping him pushed me near my physical limit. I remember that it eventually got to the point where I could hardly keep walking. I resolved to do the only thing I could think of to keep us alive and prevent our getting lost from the group: I told him that I did not have the strength to keep pushing and dragging him along, so from now on he was going to walk in front of me and if I ever caught up with him I would kick him in the rear. I know that sounds harsh, but I was getting dehydrated and low on energy. I felt that it was a life and death situation. After that it was not long before he slowed down on purpose and when I caught up, I delivered the promised kick. A little while later he did the same thing again and I kicked him a little harder. After that he stayed out in front and we just kept going. Now such methods might not be acceptable and may even be illegal, but back in those days corporal punishment was acceptable.

We walked for hours through the heat and were just barely able to keep the other people in sight. There was a long time when I all I could do was concentrate on putting one foot in front of the other without falling down. Eventually we came to a small muddy pond where the rest of the group was waiting, having arrived long before we did. I had always thought it was overly-dramatic in the movies when you see people come to a water hole and fall on their faces in the water but that is what

I did. I barely made it to the water and fell down on the edge with my face in the water. I drank a lot and splashed it all over my head. We all stayed there until we were re-hydrated and then hiked on. The whole survival hike was difficult and challenging for both the adults and the youth, but that day was the hardest for me.

There was never any more trouble with Darrell keeping up. However, one night he snuck around and stole all the food from everyone he could. Some of the kids caught him and found his stash. From a distance we saw a confrontation between Darrell and a large group of boys. Some of us thought we should go and intervene, but the leaders stopped us. "Nope. Just get over here and lay behind this bank where the kids can't see you and don't say anything."

Darrell yelled, "You're not the boss of me. I can do whatever I want, including stealing, and there is nothing you can do about it." Before long, some of the boys gathered around and beat him up. Then they warned him that if he did any more stealing, he would get more beatings. After things settled down, the leaders went back and mixed with the kids without talking about what had happened. That was the last trouble anybody had with Darrell on that trip.

We went from Coyote Canyon into Stevens Canyon then to Waterpocket Fold. We went across Waterpocket Fold and down into the Lake Powell area near the remains of the old Baker Ranch. There were times when the only available water was puddled in rock depressions and mostly dried up. Some of those puddles stunk and had bugs swimming in the water. We had nothing to purify water. I drank water that smelled and tasted so bad that I had to hold my nose while I drank and then sit and concentrate on not throwing it up.

Near Lake Powell there was plenty of good water where we camped. The BYU leader taught us how to make ash cakes with flour and water and a little salt. After mixing you just throw them in the glowing ashes of the fire until they're cooked. They were my favorite food of the whole trip. While there, each of the boys was required to have a solo experience. That meant that they had to go out and spend a night alone, away from everybody else in the group. The leaders took each boy to an isolated spot, dropped him off, told him he had to stay there and that they'd be back to pick him up the next morning. Some of the kids handled it quite well, but there were many of them who were afraid. I remember being with the leaders hearing boys out there hollering, crying and begging. The leaders told us, "Just leave them alone. This is part of the survival experience. They need to learn to overcome their fear and to take care of themselves." However, I noticed that the leaders snuck out and checked on some of the kids to make sure they were OK.

As we came to the final leg of this survival hike, it was like we were with a different group of kids. They had more courage and confidence. They were more obedient, less argumentative, and more cooperative. That week in the desert made them stronger and better in many ways.

There is much more I could tell you about that trip and there are many things that I have forgotten. I came back from that survival hike a different person than I was before. I was stronger and better than when I went out. I have remained profoundly thankful for water, food, coolness, warmth, and a comfortable bed. After I came home I filled my canteen every night and kept it on the floor next to my bed. I continued to do that for about two months.

After that first survival hike, I thought that I would never do such a thing again because it was much too hard. But as time went by, I started to have a different perspective. I saw all the growth and good aspects of it. Eventually, I started thinking that I wanted to go on more survival hikes.

The next year, a good friend and I decided we'd start a little summer business called *Rocky Mountain Sports World* to keep us busy when we weren't teaching. We bought two used twelve-passenger vans. They were painted the same. We used them as our family cars and for the business. He was the president of the Young Men in our ward and my wife was the Young Women president so those two vans took the all of the Mutual group on most of their activities.

We got business insurance and took kids on outings such as tubing and caving. The following summer I decided to take some kids on survival hikes similar to the one I had been on with the LDS Social Services/BYU. I designed the hikes to be quite a bit easier than the one I had gone on with the BYU leaders. I got detailed maps of the area that included the water sources. We had no dry camps. We did some difficult things, but nothing as punishing as the one led by the BYU experts.

The second group we took on this hike consisted of high school boys. We did not go as far as the BYU hike, and only went along the edge of Waterpocket Fold. The worst thing that happened on that hike was that one of the young men got too close to the fire one night and got a big hole burned in his jeans. Luckily, his leg wasn't burned very badly. One of the challenging things about the desert is that it is too hot in the day and too cold at night. If you only have a blanket, which is all we took, it is hard to be warm enough at night. I had a great experience with those boys and they loved it. They were strong and there weren't any of the kind of issues that we had with the day camp kids. We worked well with each other and became good friends.

Some of those boys eventually became student leaders under my supervision at the Bonneville Seminary.

On the next trip, we took a group of high school girls. Martin was my assistant on that trip. He was a high school senior and an all-around great guy. We took the girls to the same general area as the boys. On the first night we made it to Coyote Canyon and set up camp for the girls about forty yards from where Martin and I would camp that night. We told them to yell if they needed us. When we woke up next morning we were surprised to see that all of those girls had moved their bed rolls into a circle right around us.

Those young women were great and handled all the challenges well, except for their feet. We quickly discovered that most of their feet developed blisters much more easily than expected. We were well-prepared with antiseptic, band-aids, and moleskin but blistered feet were a problem throughout the hike. Some of them went barefoot part of the time. Other than the feet issues, there were no problems with the girls. They got more mentally and physically tough as the hike progressed. We eventually made it to the area where the Escalante River runs into Lake Powell. We camped for a few days there near a spring we discovered.

While we were there, Martin and I decided to do a little cliff climbing. We were not as careful as we might have been because we were climbing above water. We thought that if we slipped or needed to jump we would land harmlessly in deep water. We got out to a spot that we could not get back from and were getting ready to jump into the water. Before doing so we asked some of the girls to come and check the depth. We were surprised to find out that it was only about four feet deep. Our only option at that point was to jump, so we worked our way down to about fifteen feet above the water. When we jumped, we put our legs out in front of us so that we landed in kind of a sitting position. It hurt when we hit the water, and then the sandy bottom. Luckily, neither of us were injured.

We eventually found an easy-to-reach jump-off spot where the water was about ten feet deep. We told the young women that part of their survival experience was to jump from that point into the lake. Some of them were excited to do it, but some were afraid of heights, and others were afraid of the deep water because they were not good swimmers. Martin and I got down in the water near where they would splash down and encouraged them all to do it. Eventually, every one made the jump. We needed to help a few of them get to shallow water. After making the jump, they decided it was fun and all of them took several jumps. It turned out to be an empowering experience for them and a good lesson in overcoming fear.

There was a spot above our camp where the water from the spring ran over some cliffs and made a small waterfall about eight feet high. Surrounding trees and brush made it private. We designated this spot for the young women to shower and wash their hair. Martin and I stayed away from that area. Whatever washing we got was in the lake.

Generally, all of our survival hikes were in areas where nobody else was around, but this time was the exception. We later found out that there was a group of scouts of various ages in the area, camped far enough away that we did not know they were there. We discovered some of them had sneaked away from their camp and were trying to peek on the girls when they were showering. As soon as we found out what was going on, Martin and I crossed the river to talk with them. We explained to them that the girls needed privacy and that they needed to stay away from our camp. Considering that they were scouts, we were surprised by their response. They became very ornery and said they were going to do as they wanted related to the girls and that we could not stop them.

Martin and I told them that they needed to immediately return to their own camp and leaders and not come back. We thought that was the end of it, but when we weren't expecting it, they ambushed us. Eight of them tried to hit, kick, and tackle us. They were the weirdest bunch of scouts I have ever seen. Martin and I grabbed one after another and threw them in the river. For a while we were clearly winning, but they just kept coming at us and we started to get worn down.

One of them was big and mean. As he approached for the third time, I was not sure how much longer I could hold him off. Just as he was closing in, he got a big surprise. One of the young women came running up from behind me at angle that neither he nor I noticed. When she was about five feet away, she made a hard overhand throw of a handful of mud and rocks that hit him right in the face. He went down like a ton of bricks and started choking and coughing and rolling around. She reached down and picked up another handful of mud and rocks and several of the other girls came forward and did the same. Those boys crawled and ran away as fast as they could and we never saw them again. That was the most outstanding example of courageous action I have ever observed on a survival hike. I'll tell you, I was proud of those young women.

Overall, we had a great survival experience and they all came back stronger, better and happier than when they stared. It took more than a month for some of their feet to heal, but they never complained.

I had one more survival hike that I need to tell you about. During the summer of 1976, I went with a young man named Mac and his father, Ron. Mac was the seminary student president and he and I had become good friends. He was an outstanding student and an outstanding young man. He was a great athlete, had a black belt in karate, and was spiritually strong. He was also a great student leader.

He and I decided to go on a survival hike together and he wanted to bring his Dad. The three of us were dropped off at a place in the desert about 20 miles from Lake Powell. The plan was for his family and my wife Barbra to pick us up in a boat near the old Baker Ranch at Lake Powell. I was in my mid-twenties. Mac was eighteen and Ron was in his upper forties. We started out in an area that I had not hiked before. I was still recovering from an upper respiratory infection, but felt pretty good. We also brought along some extra food for this trip. Along with the standard things like cracked wheat, rice, flour, brown sugar, and salt, we also brought Jello, nuts, extra honey, and lots of raisins. I knew the general area and had studied the maps, but this hike turned out to be much more difficult than I expected.

The first night we were out there, we had to camp where there was no water, but we had some left in our canteens. We got camp set up and begin preparing to cook. When I went to get my food out of my pack I found that my Jello, brown sugar, raisins, honey, and nuts were all missing. I couldn't believe it. I went to Mac. "You know, something really funny has happened. I can't figure it out." I told him about the missing food.

"Oh oh," was his reply. Then he checked his pack and all of the same foods were missing. He gave me a sheepish look. "It's Dad."

"What do you mean 'It's Dad?'"

"Well, I didn't tell you this, but my dad has an eating problem. He's a compulsive eater. Sometimes he gains weight and sometimes he loses weight, but he has a hard time controlling his eating. He has probably eaten all of our best food."

I couldn't believe it. "He's your dad. Are you going to talk to him about it?"

"No. I love my dad, but he has this problem and I'm not going to talk to him about it."

"Well I'm going to talk with him about it!"

I walked over and found Ron. "Ron, did you already eat all of your best food?"

"Yup, I did."

"Did you take Mac's food?"

"Yes, I did."

"Did you take my food?"

"Yes, I did."

"Will you please give it back?"

"I can't give it back."

"Why not?"

"I already ate it all."

"You already ate all of it?"

"Yup, I did."

I barely managed to control my anger. "We're going to be out here in rough conditions for quite a while. It is going to be hard for us to survive without that food. I don't understand how you could have done this to yourself, your son, and me. Can you explain it to me?"

Ron looked at me and smiled. "If you eat the best, you got the best!"

I looked at him and didn't know what to say. I was dumbfounded. I just turned around and walked off. I went over and sat down by my pack that was missing a lot of food.

Mac came up to me. "Well, how'd it go?"

"He said, 'If you eat the best, you got the best.'" We just looked at each other and started laughing. I shrugged. "Well, I guess we'll just have to get by as well as we can."

Mac agreed, "Yup. I guess so." We did not say anything else about it for the rest of the hike, but we were more careful to watch our remaining food. Ron really was a great man but his personal weakness concerning food impacted all three of us on that hike.

The next day's hike turned out to be a lot farther and harder than we expected. Also, it quickly became apparent that I had much less strength and stamina than expected, due to my recent illness. By the time we got into the mid-afternoon, we were out of water and I was beginning to get heatstroke, which can be fatal. My head was aching, I was sick to my stomach, overheated, and having a hard time walking. At that point Mac realized what was going on with me and gave me his water.

I protested, "No, you can't do that. You need some water."

But he wouldn't take no for an answer. "I don't need it as bad as you do."

Then he started carrying my pack in addition to his. He also put my arm over his shoulder and helped support me. Mac was young, strong, and athletic. He was an amazing guy physically, mentally, and spiritually. In one way or another he carried us through that hike.

Eventually, we managed to hike our way down a steep canyon to the edge of Lake Powell, but we were on the wrong side. The spring we needed to get to was about a quarter mile across an arm of the lake and another quarter mile up a little canyon. All three of us were very thirsty and tired, and it was getting late. We considered drinking lake water, but we had nothing for purification and did not want to risk getting sick. We considering swimming across, but that seemed like too big of a risk. As we sat there trying to figure out what to do, and praying, a boat came along. We hollered and motioned for them to come over to us. They came over and asked what we wanted.

We explained our situation and asked if they would give a ride across the lake. They readily agreed.

Once we were in the boat and started across, they asked us if we wanted a cold drink. Of course we did! Their cooler was filled with nothing but beer. We politely declined their generous offer and thanked them over and over again for the ride. A few minutes later they let us out on the other side. From there it was only about a fifteen minute hike up to a deep and cool spring with lots of shade. We camped there until Mac's family came to pick us up with their boat.

The next day we went in the boat to a good place for cliff jumping into the lake. I had done some cliff jumping before but that time I made the mistake of trying a jump from much too high, about eighty feet. Mac and I jumped off at the same time. He moved in the air and positioned himself right on the way down and splashed down with no problems. The jump from that high scared me so much that I froze up, closed my eyes, and landed poorly. The water forced my legs apart and almost dislocated my hips. I went very deep and could not move my legs. Using my arms alone I just barely managed to make it to the surface. Once again, Mac came to my rescue as he helped me swim over and get into the boat.

Survival hikes proved to be a greater learning opportunity than I would have ever thought. They provided an opportunity to push beyond the boundaries of everyday experience. Hikers were able to find strength they had never had to use before. With the difficulties, there were always some really great experiences that surprised and inspired us. Pushed to the limit, a person comes to better appreciate what's really important. This experience is always profound, and reveals a person's true, and better nature. Along these paths of trial and discovery, we also managed to develop some meaningful friendships.

Lesson Insights

Survival hikes can be a microcosm of life. Learning to deal with difficult things on a more basic level can help hikers develop physical and mental strength and skill. In addition, they can learn many important things about themselves and can have significant spiritual insights.

If you are going on a physical or spiritual survival hike, make sure that you are properly prepared and that you have a qualified guide.

Discussion Questions

1. In what ways might going on a survival hike be helpful to you?
2. How well do you think you would handle a difficult survival hike?
3. Has there been anything in your life that is similar to a survival hike? What was it and what did you learn?
4. Do you have, or could you develop, the kind of courage shown by the young women on their hike? Explain.
5. Are there some things in your life that are similar to Ron's challenge? If so, what are you going to do about it?
6. What did you learn from Mac?
7. What are some other lessons you learned from this chapter?

CHAPTER 10
Uncle Mike's Passing

"And it shall come to pass that those that die in me shall not taste of death, for it shall be sweet unto them." (Doctrine and Covenants 42:46)

In August of 1975, my wife Barbra's older brother, Mike, was 30 years old. He had been quite close with Barbra and me, and our children. We visited each other often. He enjoyed our two young sons, sometimes jokingly referring to them as "the little varmints." He had a Corvette and then a Jeep, and he enjoyed taking the boys for rides. He and I shared an interest in firearms and we had fun shooting together. He had been through some frustrating things in his life and wasn't always as happy as we would have wished for him, but he had made significant progress and was becoming happier. He was not married, but he was seriously considering becoming engaged. We loved Mike, cared about him, and enjoyed our relationship with him.

We loved to listen to Mike sing and play guitar. He sang songs written by others and also wrote some wonderful songs. My favorite started with the line, "The way to see Kansas is in a fast moving car headed west," in which he sang about the difficulties he had in law school in Tennessee, then returning home to Utah somewhat discouraged but looking forward to better times. That song always touched me in an emotionally powerful way. The other songs he wrote ranged from interesting to funny, to touching. We were always excited to hear what he had just written.

The events I am now going to relate are from my point of view. Others may remember different details, but this is what happened as I remember it. August 31, 1975 was the Sunday of Labor Day weekend. We lived in South Ogden at 705 Laker View Drive. That evening, we were at home. Barbra's parents, Thelma and Howard, and her sister, Alene, were there visiting us. Thelma and Howard had gone on a weekend trip but had felt impressed to come home early. Alene had also been away and unexpectedly decided to come home early. At about 7:00 p.m., we were surprised to receive a phone call from Mike's girlfriend's brother. He said Mike was very ill and was being transported to the hospital. We hurried to McKay-Dee Hospital, which was about five minutes away.

That morning, Mike and his girlfriend, Ann, had gone to church together at their singles ward in Ogden. After church, they drove up to Morgan to visit Ann's family. They walked over to the High School track to look for Ann's little sister. They talked as they jogged around the track. Then Mike decided to sprint. After a short distance, he slowed and went to lay on the grass. Ann came and sat down beside him. She noticed that he did not look well. He complained, "I feel sick. I feel bad." He looked over her shoulder at the sky and asked, "Is that a plane or a star?" Ann turned to look behind her and didn't see anything. When she turned back around, Mike was unconscious.

She was not able to wake him. She called for an ambulance, which came and transported him from Morgan to the hospital. We arrived at the hospital a few minutes after the ambulance. They took us to a waiting room and asked us to stay there. They explained that it was very serious, that they would be working on him, and that they would let us know anything they could as soon as possible. This came as a shock to all of us. Mike hadn't been ill and had seemed to be in good health. He'd had some irregularities in his heartbeat, but it wasn't considered to be a serious problem.

I was uncomfortable staying in the waiting room and not being near Mike. I was also concerned about whether or not he had received a priesthood blessing. I left the waiting room and found a back way into the emergency room area without being noticed. Back then, hospitals were not as carefully monitored as they are now. There was a lot of activity behind a particular curtain. I very quietly slipped into the next enclosed area, which was empty and somewhat dark. I went over to the corner where I could see and hear what was going on.

Several nurses and at least two doctors were working on Mike. I didn't know what they had done previously and I didn't understand everything they were doing then. There was a lot of equipment around Mike. A rapid discussion was going on, and there was a feeling of great urgency. They prepared to shock Mike to try to get his heart started. The doctor held electronic paddles and gave instructions. Mike lay on the table with no clothing from the waist up. His arms hung down on each side of the table. I could see no signs of life. It was not long before the doctor said, "Clear," and held the paddles to Mike's chest. A shock caused Mike's arms to raise in the air. They stopped and looked at the heart monitor. The line appeared to be flat and there were no bleeps. They watched for a short time, then the doctor ordered, "Let's give it another shot." They applied the paddles. Once again, the doctor shouted, "Clear," and the shock was administered. Mike's body reacted as before. They stopped, waited, and watched the monitor. Once again there was no change. They waited a short time and administered the shock a third time. Once again the doctors and nurses watched all the equipment and the monitors. Others listened to his chest with stethoscopes. Then the doctor set down his paddles and looked sadly around at the people in the room. "I'm sorry. I think we've done all we can." He then looked at his watch and declared the time of death. Someone wrote it down. They milled around a little bit, secured some of the equipment, partially covered Mike, and soon left the room. They went down the hall without seeing me.

Beginning the moment we heard there was a serious problem, we had been doing a lot of praying. We had a family prayer together in the waiting room before I left. Throughout that time and while I was secretly watching, I was very anxious to give Mike a blessing. After the medical personnel left, I slipped out of my hiding place and went to Mike. I closed the curtain so that Mike and I were alone. I was determined to give him a blessing. That may sound unusual because he had already been pronounced dead, but I believed in the power of priesthood blessings, even in extreme situations.

About six months into my mission, I was in Oceanside, California. My companion and I were called to a man's house very near where we lived to give him a blessing. We hurried right over. When we got there, he appeared to be having a heart attack. He was lying on the floor having convulsions, and had turned purple. We quickly gave him a blessing, which was difficult with the convulsions. Immediately after the blessing, he quit convulsing, became calm, and began to breathe normally. His color returned to normal and he sat up and conversed with us. He told us that he felt much better and was very grateful. We left shortly thereafter and he continued to be well.

I had read in the scriptures and had heard stories about miraculous healings. I believed in Christ's power and the priest-hood. However, that blessing in Oceanside was the first blessing I remember participating in. I had faith that healings could happen but had never observed or experienced it prior to that time in Oceanside. After that experience I had opportunities to be involved in many blessings. Most of them seemed to be what may be called normal. You give people a blessing and there's nothing too dramatic about it. Most of the time the people receive medical treatment, and most of the time they get better. It is easy to wonder if they got better because of the medical treatment, because of the blessing, or both.

I had another experience in the mission field with a family in the Glendora area. I think their name was Marlow. We had taught this family and they had all been baptized. We cared about and loved them. Shortly after the baptism, the nine-year-old daughter became very sick with a kidney infection. Her mother was a nurse. The kidney infection had been diagnosed and medication prescribed. The treatment did not seem to be helping. Her fever was very high. The mother had talked with the doctors, who said, "Okay, we'll give it one more night and if she is not better in the morning, bring her to the hospital."

That family didn't know much about blessings, but they asked us if we would give her one. I performed the sealing part of the blessing. Whenever I gave a blessing I always tried to be in tune with the Lord, clear my mind, and speak whatever I felt was given by the Spirit. In that particular blessing, I felt the Spirit very strongly. I felt very specifically guided in what I was saying. I blessed the little girl that she would get better very quickly without additional medical treatment. I also told her that she and her family had done the right thing in getting baptized and that her healing was a special blessing that was coming to her and to her family in connection with joining the church. We left their home shortly after giving the blessing.

I was very upset because I had never given a blessing that was that specific and that involved those kinds of promises. Back at our apartment, I quickly went and knelt down to talk with the Lord. I spent more than an hour praying. I pleaded with the Lord to heal that little girl and help the blessing to come true.

The next day, we talked with the family and asked about the little girl. Her mother said, "Oh, it's wonderful. Right after you left, her fever broke. Her symptoms have disappeared. I've been in touch with the doctor and we feel that there's no need for her to go to the hospital."

I saw the power of Christ, the priesthood, and faith many more times in the mission field and thereafter. By the time of this incident with Mike, I had graduated from college and had been teaching seminary for a few years. I was very familiar with what the scriptures say about blessings and healing. I'd had opportunities to give many blessings. I had felt the power of the Lord and had seen miraculous healings.

As I entered the room where Mike lay, I decided, "I'm going to go ahead and give him this blessing." I knew from the scriptures and from church history that people have occasionally been raised from the dead. I had faith that Mike could be raised from the dead. I thought that it was an important time in his life and there were many blessings in store for him here. I thought, "His life is headed the right way and he's looking forward to marriage. This is not the right time for him to die. I'm here and I'm just going to lay my hands on his head and give him a blessing. I'm going to command that he be healed and that he be raised up and brought back to life." I approached Mike with no doubt in my mind.

I was also very emotional because of my relationship with Mike and his relationship with the rest of the family. As I approached to give him the blessing I had a strong feeling that I should not do so. I was so anxious to give him the blessing and so emotionally involved that I just brushed off the feeling and kept moving toward him. Once again, I had a strong feeling that I should not bless him. I hesitated and stood there, but again brushed off the feeling and took the last step toward Mike. As I reached out my hands to lay them on his head and try to bring him back to life, I was hit with a spiritual force that made me stagger and knocked me back. At the same time, strong words came into my mind. "No! Do not give him a blessing. You are attempting to step beyond your bounds. What's happening here is beyond your authority." Other powerful words, thoughts and feelings came. It was a spiritual rebuke stronger than I had ever felt in my life. I have never felt anything quite like that before or since.

It was made abundantly clear to me that I was not to attempt to give Mike a blessing, nor command him to arise from the dead. The thoughts and feelings I was having were wrong for that particular time and circumstance. I was surprised, dumbfounded. I staggered, clearly understanding that Lord did not want me to proceed and that He was upset with me. He had told me two times, and the third time he made sure I got the point. Even though I did not like it, I understood that Mike was dead and was going to stay dead. There was nothing that I could or should do about it. I was overwhelmed with grief and began to cry almost uncontrollably. After a few minutes I quietly slipped out of the emergency room and went back to the waiting room with the family.

Right after I got there, the doctor came to tell us that he was very sorry, that they had done all they could, but that Mike had passed away. Of course there was a lot of surprise and grief. It was a very difficult time for all of us.

Mike's mother asked me if I would be one of the main speakers at the funeral. I wasn't sure I could, but she felt very strongly that I should speak. I had a tremendous spiritual struggle for several days because I was very upset about Mike dying. I was unable to reconcile in my mind that it was the right time for him to die. I was also hurting from the spiritual rebuke I had received. It was a very emotionally and spiritually challenging time.

My grandparents all died when I was quite young. Mike's passing was the first time in my life that I was old enough to personally deal with the death of a loved one. It was very difficult for me. I studied and prayed intently. I found several books on death and the spirit world. During the next few days, I spent many hours thinking, praying, reading and studying.

By the day of the funeral, I had received a new and different kind of testimony than I had ever had before. I knew that it was Mike's time to die. I knew that the Lord was always aware of and involved in the death of a righteous person. I also learned that not all death is in accordance with the Lord's will. There are things that happen in mortality because of agency and the choices people make. I knew then, and I know now that there are many things that can affect the time of death. I also learned at that time that the Lord is involved in the circumstances of people dying, especially if the people have received the fullness of the Gospel and if the blessings of the priesthood are involved. I didn't learn about every death and about all circumstances but I did learn at that time, that it was in fact Mike's appointed time to go into the spirit world. I received a testimony that it was in accordance with the will of the Lord and that Mike's progress and mission would continue there.

I also received a testimony that Mike would not be deprived of the blessings of an eternal marriage and that he would receive every blessing promised the righteous. I also came to know that those things would be accomplished in the spirit world and through temple work. I received that testimony and knew that this was the will of the Lord. Receiving that testimony was similar to the way other testimonies are gained, such as knowing that Christ is the Savior, that the Book of Mormon is true, and that the Gospel has been restored. I had a testimony of all those things and during that time between Mike's death and his funeral, the Lord communed with me and answered my prayers. He helped me to know and understand that even though this was difficult for all of us, it was part of the Lord's plan. Mike was happy and would continue to be happy in the spirit world. He wouldn't lose any blessings. In fact, his blessings would be increased.

After receiving that testimony and conviction, I spoke at the funeral. I knew that I was intellectually and spiritually prepared to give that talk. When I got up and attempted to speak, I quickly discovered that I was not emotionally prepared: I cried through most of it. However, I was able to contain my emotions enough to give the talk that I felt the Lord wanted me to give. I told the people that even though it was difficult for us, I had received a testimony that this was Mike's time to go and that the Lord took him intentionally at that time. I did not tell about my experience at the hospital, but I did talk about the struggle I had reconciling his death and shared some of the stories and scriptures that I had studied. I was later told that my talk gave great comfort to the family and others who cared about Mike.

A few weeks later, Barbra was of course still missing Mike and mourning his not being there. During that time, he came to her in a dream. They hugged. She told me how the hug felt "real." It did not feel like a dream to her. It felt like Mike was actually there. In the dream, she felt close to him and the Spirit of the Lord was very strong. When she woke up, she distinctly remembered the dream. It has always been a source of great comfort to her.

It has been many years, but I still remember these things very clearly. I'm grateful that the Lord blessed me to be able to understand that situation and to be comforted at the time of Mike's death, and to know that it happened in accordance with the will of the Lord. I learned and felt things at that time that have been a blessing to me and to many others throughout my life. I have learned by experience that the power of Christ through his priesthood is real and that it includes power over life and death, but only if it's in accordance with the will of the Lord.

Discussion Questions

1. Have you or someone you know well experienced a miraculous healing?
2. If so, what effect did it have on the people involved?
3. What do you need to do in order to be spiritually prepared for the death of a loved one?
4. How can you prepare to be more submissive to the Lord's will in any difficult situation?

CHAPTER 11
Who Is Most Important?

"Fathers, provoke not your children to anger, lest they be discouraged."
(Colossians 3:21)

During the time we lived in New Mexico I was called to serve as the stake Young Men's president. One year the there was a stake dance held in the town near us where the stake center was located. I was not in charge of that dance but I attended along with a good size group of youth from our ward.

It seemed to me that things at the dance went well. However, some complaints were made to the stake presidency concerning several possible dress standard violations, as well as several other issues. One of those concerns involved our son. A song played at the dance was the instrumental "Tequila." That song had been featured in a movie called Pee-wee's Big Adventure (1985) wherein Pee-wee Herman performed a funny dance to the music, dancing on a table top. When the song started my oldest son spontaneously jumped up on a table and did a hilarious imitation of that dance to much laughter and applause.

Subsequent to the dance the stake presidency issued a directive cancelling all stake youth dances citing, among other things, dress standards, music selection, and my son's table dance. I wrote them a letter suggesting that stake dances be allowed to continue with more clearly defined rules and increased supervision. The stake presidency accepted my suggestion. The next stake dance was scheduled to be held at the Institute of Religion, under my supervision.

My son, who was a high school senior at that time, accepted the responsibility of setting up all the music and lighting. He worked long and hard, including several hours before the dance, trying to make sure everything was appropriate and well done. Not long before the dance was scheduled to start there was a technical glitch. He was finally able to solve the problem a few minutes after the dance was supposed to start. He turned on the music and headed for the door to go home and change into appropriate dance attire. As he crossed the floor a young lady asked him to dance. Even though he knew he wasn't dressed as the guidelines dictated, he thought she might feel bad if he declined so he accepted her request. A short time later, unaware of the situation, I came from working on something else to check on things on the dance floor and was embarrassed and upset by what I saw.

As soon as that song was over I quickly took my son into my office and chastised him. I forcefully told him that dancing in his work clothes had embarrassed us all and that he was risking the re-cancellation of all youth dances. As soon as he left I had a very bad feeling. At that point I prayed asking to know what was wrong and seeking confirmation that I was handling things correctly. I was surprised when this question came clearly into my mind: "Who is most important?" Of course I knew the right answer was not "me." I responded, "All these young men and women." Silence. Then I tried, "The Stake Presidency." Silence. Then it hit me. "My son." Immediately the spirit rushed into my mind and heart.

A short time later my son returned to the dance dressed appropriately. I asked if I could speak to him in my office and he reluctantly entered. With tears in my eyes I told him, how sorry I was, how much I loved and appreciated him, and how grateful I was that he was my son. He smiled, and I was shocked to hear him say, "For a while there I thought I had lost my best friend." We hugged and cried, and then he went happily into the dance.

Discussion Questions

1. Why wasn't it obvious to me that my son was doing the best he could in a very difficult situation? How could this insight apply to you?

2. In your opinion, what is the lesson I learned and how may it have affected the rest of my life? How might it apply to your life?

CHAPTER 12
Faith, Not Fear

"And the same day, when the even was come, he saith unto them, Let us pass over unto the other side. And when they had sent away the multitude, they took him even as he was in the ship. And there were also with him other little ships. And there arose a great storm of wind, and the waves beat into the ship, so that it was now full. And he was in the hinder part of the ship, asleep on a pillow: and they awake him, and say unto him, Master, carest thou not that we perish? And he arose, and rebuked the wind, and said unto the sea, Peace, be still. And the wind ceased, and there was a great calm. And he said unto them, Why are ye so fearful? how is it that ye have no faith? And they feared exceedingly, and said one to another, What manner of man is this, that even the wind and the sea obey him?" (Mark 4:35-41)

The Sea of Galilee is about seven miles wide and twice as long. It is the lowest freshwater lake on earth. About 65 miles to the south lies the famous saltwater Dead Sea, the lowest lake on earth. Both lakes are fed by the Jordan River. The Sea of Galilee is about 30 miles east of the Mediterranean Sea and about 700 feet below sea level. Because of its geographical circumstances, the Sea of Galilee is subject to sudden and fierce wind storms. Between April and October there is very little rainfall. In his account of the calming of the sea Mark specifically says that it was a great storm of wind. (Mark 4:37) Most pictures and videos mistakenly show rain.

When the windstorm occurred, they were probably in Peter's fishing boat. (See GVS, *Concise Harmony of the Four Gospels*, 25, note 30.) Peter, and at least three other disciples, were experienced mariners. As the storm continued, so much water had splashed into the boat that they were in danger of sinking. Jesus must have been very tired and sleeping soundly. By the time they woke him, even the seasoned fishermen were in a state of panic.

When Jesus arose and calmed the sea, he demonstrated power over the elements and weather. Thereafter, instead of just saying some comforting words, Jesus admonished them, saying, "Why are ye so fearful? how is it that ye have no faith?" It appears that Jesus was using this incident as a powerful object lesson to teach his disciples that they needed to learn to live by faith, not fear. He wanted them to understand that they did not need to live in fear. He tried to help them understand that they could overcome or endure the storms of life by using the power of their faith.

It is also interesting to note that this incident is a partial fulfillment of the Messianic prophesy found in Psalms 107:19-20, 28-29, which says, "Then they cry unto the Lord in their trouble, and he saveth them out of their distresses. He sent his word, and healed them, and delivered them from their destructions... Then they cry unto the Lord in their trouble, and he bringeth them out of their distresses. He maketh the storm a calm, so that the waves thereof are still."

I would like to share an experience I had related to Mark 4:35-41. When I was teaching seminary and institute in New Mexico, there was an older sister named Gail who attended institute class. She had experienced some of the effects of sin, grief, and sorrow in her life. She was converted to the gospel when she was older. She was the only one in her family who was converted, except her son, David. At the time of this account he was in his early thirties and had recently been released from prison.

Gail did well in her church and institute attendance and in being a disciple of Christ. I became friends with her and David. I helped him with some spiritual issues and he helped me with some computer issues. Eventually, she became very ill and was diagnosed with late stage cancer. The doctors said that her cancer was terminal. She received treatment, which was not effective. Finally, they sent her home to die.

One day, David called me. "Will you come out to the house and give my mother a blessing?"

"Yes I will, but it might be better if your bishop or home teacher did it."

He insisted, "No, we want you."

I took one of my sons and went to their home. When David opened the door, we felt a very negative feeling in the house. He invited us in and led us to his mother. We passed others of her family who all glared at us. David escorted us into the room where his mother was. Half a dozen family members followed us. They all wore harsh, mean expressions. I could tell that they were angry that we were there. I think it was because they didn't like the Church of Jesus Christ of Latter-day Saints.

Gail lay on the bed, unconscious, but thrashing around. She moaned and cried, threw her arms and legs around and rolled from sided to side. It was shocking and horrible. She seemed to be suffering greatly. David repeated his request for a blessing for her. I suggested that it would be best if the others in the room left during the blessing. I did that because it is more difficult to feel the Spirit when surrounded with negativity. However, they refused to leave.

We had a hard time anointing her head with the oil because she was jerking so much. When I laid my hands on her head, it was difficult to hang on. As I started to give the blessing, a strange thing occurred that has never happened to me on any other occasion. Even though my eyes were closed, in my mind it seemed like I was high above her. It seemed like my arms got very long and my hands went far down to where she was. Then it seemed like I actually descended down to where she was, with my hands still on her head. Then, I was there with her. She and I were on a boat in a fierce storm. I wondered what in the world was going on? I had never even heard about anything like that before. It was like I was in her nightmare. I was surrounded by wind, water and fear.

I wondered what was going to happen and what I was supposed to do. Then suddenly it came to me. I knew where I was and what to do. With the power and authority of Christ I commanded, "Peace, be still." Instantly, everything was calm. There was no more storm or fear. Gail immediately quit thrashing around and lay very still and calm.

I finished the blessing with an explanation that storms can be physical, mental, emotional, or spiritual. I blessed her to be at peace with the Lord, that she would see him soon, and that all would be well. When I ended the blessing, took my hands off her head, and opened my eyes, I looked down and she was lying there just as peacefully as could be. There was a feeling of great peace over the whole room. I looked at the family members. Their eyes were wide and they were stunned. We all knew something miraculous had happened. They did not understand, but they felt the power. David and I hugged.

He told us thanks and we left. Gail lay there peacefully for a few more hours, and then she passed away.

That experience gave me a new depth and breath of understanding. When I read Mark 4:35-41 before that, I always visualized things on the outside, not the inside. Sometimes the storms we have are from external things. Sometimes, the storms we have—the mountains of grief and the oceans of sorrow—are on the inside. But here's the thing—whether it's on the inside or the outside, Jesus can heal it. He can calm it. Even if somebody is going to die, there can be peace.

The hymn, "Master, The Tempest Is Raging," is a wonderful song about this. The text was written by Maryann Baker and the music by H.R. Palmer, who both obviously had a deep understanding of these things. This song encompasses everything that we've discussed.

Now let's return to the New Testament setting at the Sea of Galilee a few months after the previous account, near the time of the Passover Feast. Jesus taught and demonstrated another lesson about having faith, not fear.

> And straightway Jesus constrained his disciples to get into a ship, and to go before him unto the other side, while he sent the multitudes away. And when he had sent the multitudes away, he went up into a mountain apart to pray: and when the evening was come, he was there alone. But the ship was now in the midst of the sea, tossed with waves: for the wind was contrary. And in the fourth watch of the night Jesus went unto them, walking on the sea. And when the disciples saw him walking on the sea, they were troubled, saying, It is a spirit; and they cried out for fear. But straightway Jesus spake unto them, saying, Be of good cheer; it is I; be not afraid. And Peter answered him and said, Lord, if it be thou, bid me come unto thee on the water. And he said, Come. And when Peter was come down out of the ship, he walked on the water, to go to Jesus.

But when he saw the wind boisterous, he was afraid; and beginning to sink, he cried, saying, Lord, save me. And immediately Jesus stretched forth his hand, and caught him, and said unto him, O thou of little faith, wherefore didst thou doubt? And when they were come into the ship, the wind ceased. Then they that were in the ship came and worshipped him, saying, Of a truth thou art the Son of God. (Matthew 14:22-33)

Note that the disciples in the boat were trying to return to Capernaum on the northwest end of the Sea of Galilee and that they were attempting to go against the wind. It is possible that they were using the sailing technique known as tacking, but they were probably trying to row the boat into the wind, an extremely difficult and tiring task. When Jesus finally went to them, it was the forth watch of the night, meaning that it was between 3:00 a.m. and 6:00 a.m. They had been struggling for at least seven hours.

By walking on the water, Jesus demonstrated his power over astronomic physical forces, including electromagnetic force, nuclear force, and gravity. Jesus had probably been walking over the waves for miles before he approached the boat. When the disciples first saw him, they were afraid that he was a ghost. One might wonder how they could see him during the night. In fact, some pseudo-intellectual types have used this issue as an excuse not to believe this account. However, we know that this circumstance occurred at about the time of the Passover Feast, which happens every year during the first full moon after the Vernal (Spring) Equinox. They could have seen him on the water during a windstorm because the moon was full.

Note that one of the first things Jesus did was to tell them not to be afraid. Consider Peter's assertive, courageous desire and behavior in attempting to walk on the water with Jesus. However, he was distracted by the boisterous wind, became afraid, and slowly began to sink. There was time to cry for help, and for Jesus to reach out and lift him up. Of course, part of the message is that we need to ask for and reach out for divine help in order to be saved. Another part of the lesson is that we need to resist being defeated by fear. One of the most important things to observe is that Peter was being supported by his own faith. It was not just Jesus supporting him. When his faith wavered he began to sink. Of course we need to rely on Jesus. In addition to that, we need to think, feel and live by our own faith.

In both of these lessons on the Sea of Galilee, Jesus is teaching his disciples, both then and now, that we need to live by **faith, not fear**.

Discussion Questions

1. If you have been in a dangerous situation, how were you saved?
2. How have faith and fear been operative in your life?
3. What did you learn from the experience with Gail, and how can you apply it in your life.
4. What did you learn from the "walking on water" account, and how can it help you?

CHAPTER 13
Saved from Freezing

In the fall of 1989, our family was living in New Mexico. I served as the CES coordinator for several stakes, which included all the early morning seminary classes in that area. I taught an early morning seminary class with about fifty students, and I was the institute director and instructor.

Prior to being transferred there, we lived in Farmington, Utah in a wonderful house. Moving to New Mexico was a great blessing, but also a great sacrifice for our family, partly because our extended family and close friends all lived on the Wasatch Front in Utah. There were other sacrifices involved, but we felt very blessed that the Lord had given us the opportunity to return to teaching after being out of the Church Educational System for a few years.

There were many good people in that New Mexico town, and our ward was a great blessing to us. While we were there, one of my sons played quarterback on the high school football team. He was a very good player but didn't get a lot of playing time. The circumstances surrounding this were strange. If he made the slightest mistake, he was immediately jerked out of the game. On the other hand, if he made an excellent play, he was also quickly pulled off the field. We couldn't figure it out because it simply did not make sense. It was obvious that his abilities were greater than any of the others who were playing in that position. He had a good attitude, worked hard, and accepted coaching, but somehow he spent the majority of his time on the sidelines. This was especially hard on our son because at that point in his life, football was very important to him.

After this had gone on for a good part of the season, one of the assistant football coaches came to see me in my office. He was a nice guy who was a member of our ward. On the condition that I keep it confidential, he explained that the problem had more to do with racial discrimination than football. (My son was one of only a few white players on a predominantly Latino team.)

Without going into details, let me just say that it was painful to watch my son going through this challenge. I prayed about what I could do. I was unable to come up with a solution that felt right, other than counseling my son to do the best he could, knowing that there was something going on that had nothing to do with him or his abilities.

One evening, the high school football team had a late season home game. My son got in the game and made a fantastic play. The coach immediately pulled him out of the game and did not play him any more. Mostly due to poor quarterback play, they lost the game as they had many others. Our family all felt deeply disappointed and upset.

After the game, our son told us that he was going to ride home with some friends, so we went home and expected him to arrive fairly soon. The weather had turned very cold and snow was accumulating quickly. When he didn't come home after a while, we began to wonder where he was. After about two hours, we were very worried. I called one of his friends to ask if he knew where our son was. He said he did not, but something in his voice did not ring true to me. I waited a while longer, then called back and asked to speak with his father. They lived in a neighboring ward. I knew he was a very good man, and a medical doctor. I explained to him that we were very concerned not knowing where our son was in the harsh weather. I told him that I suspected his son knew something that he had not told me about the whereabouts of my son. I asked him if he could help. He said that he would try and then call me back.

A few minutes later, he called back and said that he had talked with his son and with some persuasion, his son had told him that he knew something about where my missing son was. He had left the high school with a group of kids whom he didn't know very well. They were going to drive around for a while and then go to a party. He told me some of the kid's names and where the party was supposed to be. I thanked the doctor and his son and hung up. Then I got in my car and drove up to where the party was supposed to be. The location was only about a half-mile from our house.

I drove by a few times and looked for our son but couldn't see him, so I went to the door and asked if he was there. They told me he wasn't. I asked if they knew where he was and they said they didn't. I couldn't get them to tell me anything else and they were not very friendly. I could tell that there was some drinking going on and I became even more worried about my son. I drove around in the area, and I prayed.

After some time, I went home and told my wife what I had found out. We knelt in prayer together for our son. Then I told her that I didn't know what else to do, except to continue driving around looking and praying for him.

Eventually, I drove by the house of his friend. The house was dark and there was no car in the driveway. I started to drive up the street on the south side of the house but I could not make it because it was too steep and slippery. I backed down the road and drove around the block, coming down the street that was too slippery to go up. At the corner, I turned and started to drive away. Then I had a distinct feeling that I should try again to go back up the slippery road. I backed the car up and tried to get a run to get up the street. As I was struggling to drive up there, my son suddenly ran into the headlights about thirty yards away. He was not wearing his jacket or shoes. He was waving his arms and running through the snow. Then suddenly he collapsed right in the middle of the road. I could not get the car to him because it was so slippery, so I jumped out and ran. When I got to him, he was semi-conscious. I half-carried, half-dragged him back to the car.

During all of this, Barbra was understandably upset. She was at home, angry and getting angrier, because our son had not come home as agreed. Fear played a part in her feelings as she stewed and worried about where he was and whether or not he was safe. This was before the days when cell phones were available, so during my search, she did not know what was happening. She had prayed about the situation, but our son was still not home and no comfort had come to her. In desperation, she knelt and prayed again, and continued to do so for over thirty minutes, expressing her anger, frustration and fear to the Lord, asking for help to deal with the situation better and begging that our son would return home safely. Her prayer was answered in a dramatic way. Her anger and fear melted away and she knew what she had to do. If our son did come home, and she was assured that he would, she knew that she could not lash out at him with angry or accusing words. Expressing the worry and fear that she had been filled with would not help the situation. The answer and thought that came to her was that she should hug him and tell him that she loved him. That was all. Her ability to do that came directly from the Lord. That was not what she had felt like doing, but it was what she was enabled to do when he arrived home. We later found out that her loving response in that very distressing situation had a significant impact on our son.

I turned the heater up full-blast and raced home. I managed to get him into the house. He partially revived, received Barbra's hug and message of love, and mumbled something before passing out again. We immediately called that same doctor and asked him what to do. He said he would be there in minutes. We dried our son off and tried to get him warm. Even though it was about 11:00 p.m., the doctor got there very quickly. He examined our son and said he did not have frostbite, but was suffering from hypothermia. He instructed us to cover him with blankets and told me to get in bed with him and hold him to help him get warmed up. The doctor said that he expected him to recover soon. It was a very emotional experience to hold my son while he shivered uncontrollably. I was filled with gratitude that the Lord had miraculously helped me find my son and save his life.

There is no need to relate all of the details, but my son later told me that he had been feeling very depressed about football. The guys he was riding with that night were not his friends. They kicked him out of the car at his friend's house. Nobody was home and he could not get inside. It only took minutes before he was very cold, so he climbed in their camper to try to get warm. There were no sleeping bags or blankets in the camper so he got colder and colder by the minute. His feet got really cold, so he took off his shoes to try and rub his feet to get them warm, but it didn't work. He was not thinking clearly and could not decide what to do. He was up in the top part of the camper that goes over the truck cab. He glanced out the window and saw our car drive slowly by. He scrambled out of the camper and ran to the road before passing out in front of the headlights as I was coming back.

I have found that it is easier to cope with someone who is hurting you than to cope with someone who is hurting one of your children. I became quite wrought up about the whole situation. I wanted to expose those responsible for hurting and endangering my son by discriminating against him. I wanted justice. I had several ideas but none of them seemed right. I spent quite a bit of time praying about it. I finally realized that I was becoming consumed with feelings of anger and resentment. Eventually, I decided that I needed to turn it over to the Lord, forgive those who were involved the best that I could, and leave everything else up to the Lord. When I finally was able to do that, the burden was lifted. A very interesting thing happened after that: the head football coach and all of his assistants were fired at the end of that losing season. I have always wondered if the Lord had something to do with that.

I compiled a highlight film of our son's great plays and passed it on to the college coaches. My son received a football scholarship, graduated from high school early, and immediately started attending college.

Discussion Questions

1. What do you think is the best way to deal with people or situations that are discriminatory or unfair?
2. Can you identify some parenting principles related to this chapter that you are interested in applying in your life?
3. How has the Lord helped save you or someone you love (physically or spiritually)?
4. Why is it important to be practiced and proficient in prayer and following the Spirit?

CHAPTER 14
He Never Talked to Me

"Yea, we see that whosoever will may lay hold upon the word of God, which is quick and powerful, which shall divide asunder all the cunning and the snares and the wiles of the devil, and lead the man of Christ in a strait and narrow course across that everlasting gulf of misery which is prepared to engulf the wicked—" (Helaman 3:29)

This chapter tells the story of an unusual student and my experiences with him in 1992. As I describe what happened, I will quote his actual words from papers he handed in, which I have saved for more than 23 years. (At that time, I was having my students do more writing than I normally did in seminary). I shared this account with other seminary and institute teachers many years later when I was asked to make a presentation in a Church Educational System (CES) teacher training seminar in Utah.

Brian Brown never said one word to me. Whenever I talked to him, or asked him a question, he would just look down and scowl or look the other way. He spoke with other people just fine but refused to speak to me. He did, however, write many things to me.

When there were writing assignments, Brian wrote notes to me instead of doing the assignments. The first thing he wrote at the beginning of the year was, "My parents made me take this class but it's not like I'm ever going to use it. I don't like you and I don't like this class."

On the next assignment sheet he wrote, "Seminary in your class is no privilege. It's a punishment from my parents. Why don't you go back to where you came from? All, or most all of your students hate you and your stupid rules and your inability to have any fun."

Later he wrote, "I, Brian Brown, know that this is really a stupid class because of the stupid teacher with his stupid spiritual experiences and this assignment is stupid too."

In the teacher training seminar, I asked the teachers what they would have done in a situation like that. The first answer was to have a talk with his parents and bishop. I explained that I did try to talk with his parents but they had very little to say over the phone and declined to meet with me in person. When I talked to Brian's bishop, he said that this was a difficult situation and he didn't think that anything he could do would help. The bottom line was that I was on my own with this kid.

In the teacher training class, they suggested several other things. I explained that I tried to talk with him in class, in the hall, and in my office with no success. He just ignored me. Communication with the parents was out. Communication with the bishop was out. Nothing was suggested that I had not tried, but still there was no improvement in the situation. Then I asked the teachers to continue to think about how they would handle a similar student in one of their classes as I read more things that Brian wrote to me.

On another assignment he wrote, "So you played running back? You look like a guard, a guard for the water. You played at Weber. What conference is that? The BFC—The Bald and Fat Conference? And you think being a goody-goody will make you happy? Huh? Well, maybe you should read the scriptures for once and know that it is wrong to lie. Being a goody-goody ain't gonna mean you're gonna be happy. It means you're gonna be a nothing."

On a later assignment there was a question which asked, "What's wrong with 2 Nephi 28:7-9, where it says, 'Eat, drink and be merry, for tomorrow we die?'" His answer to that was, "Because we might get as fat as our seminary teacher."

Another assignment included this question, "What suffering and difficulties are you encountering at this time?" His answer was, "This stupid class and this stupid teacher and my stupid parents for making me take this stupid class with this stupid teacher." The same assignment also included a question referring to Mosiah 7:33 where it talks about being delivered from bondage if you turn to the Lord. The question was: "Likening this challenge unto yourself, what specific things can you do to throw off any of the bondage that you might be experiencing?" He answered, "I could ditch seminary and go be a stoner at the bridge, so I won't have to listen to this bull." At that particular high school, the kids who were into drugs and alcohol, etc. sometimes ditched classes and hung out at the bridge that was located across the street from the high school, which was near the seminary building.

On a later assignment he didn't even respond to the questions and simply wrote, "You're about as stupid and boring as your jokes." Another time he wrote, "I wish you would stop talking about your spiritual experiences. It's really annoying me." A different time he wrote, "I think you should quit trying to teach. If you can't teach right, don't teach at all."

In the teacher training seminar, I asked the teachers, "If one of your students said things like this to you how would it make you feel?" At this point, some of the younger teachers were exhibiting signs of stress. They became visibly upset as we discussed having to deal with such a student. Never in their wildest dreams had they ever imagined that being a seminary teacher would expose them to that kind of ridicule and abuse.

If I had had this kind of experience early in my teaching career, I might have had more self-doubts. Thankfully, this experience happened after many years of successful teaching. I had been around enough to know that most students responded well to me. I felt like some of the things he wrote were actually quite funny.

Even though all my efforts to reach Brian had failed, I still needed to deal with the situation. I prayed, pondered, and waited. I finally decided that I was not going to respond in a negative way to the things that this young man said. I was just going to ignore it. I decided that I would treat him as kindly as I treated any other student and that I would try to avoid any kind of confrontation or negative experience. I didn't try to drag him into my office. I didn't try to kick him out of my class. I didn't try to make him talk to me. I decided that I would just be nice and say pleasant things. I decided to say "Hello" to him even if he never said one word to me. I would be polite. I would go on being nice and just continue on as though he had never written the notes. I decided I would apply the following counsel from Brigham Young:

> One of the nicest things in the world is to let an enemy alone entirely, and it mortifies him to death. If your neighbors talk about you, and you think that they do wrong in speaking evil of you, do not let them know that you ever heard a word, and conduct yourselves as if they always did right, and it will mortify them, and they will say, "We'll not try this game any longer." (GVS, *The Best of Joseph and Brigham*, 179)

And that's just what I did.

In the second week of the second term, there was an assignment concerning scripture reading, scripture mastery, service, and self-evaluation. On it he wrote, "Since when are we supposed to have homework in this stupid class? I don't care if you kick me out of your class. I'm really only in it because my parents make me. I'm really tired of hearing about all your stupid spiritual experiences and why do you have to be so exact about everything? We're not all perfect like you are and so don't expect us to be as perfect as you are."

In the middle of the second term, he turned in an assignment that had no response except in the place where students were to write in their Book of Mormon personal reading point. There he wrote "Alma chapter 44." I wondered if he might actually be reading the Book of Mormon. Of course, I knew that great things happen in the minds and hearts of those who sincerely read the Book of Mormon. For the first time I began to feel hope for him.

The very next assignment included questions based on Helaman 3:27-29 which says, "Thus we may see that the Lord is merciful unto all who will, in the sincerity of their hearts, call upon his holy name. Yea, thus we see that the gate of heaven is open unto all, even to those who will believe on the name of Jesus Christ, who is the Son of God. Yea, we see that whosoever will may lay hold upon the word of God, which is quick and powerful, which shall divide asunder all the cunning and the snares and the wiles of the devil, and lead the man of Christ in a strait and narrow course across that everlasting gulf of misery which is prepared to engulf the wicked—" Here are some of the answers he wrote:

"Everlasting gulf of misery."

"Quick and powerful."

"The cunning and snares of the devil."

In response to another question, he wrote the names of several people in a particular part of the Book of Mormon, with a short description of who they were.

I was amazed. There were no insults, no negative comments. He was reading the Book of Mormon and something was changing.

The next assignment was a multiple choice worksheet from the manual. As I quickly looked over the one he handed in, I observed that most of the answers were correct.

After that, there was a test that included questions on some previously covered parts of the Book of Mormon. One of the questions was, "List six characteristics of Moroni from Alma chapter 48." Brian wrote, "One, he worked hard for the welfare and safety of his people, two, he was firm in his faith in Christ, three, he had perfect understanding, four, he was a man who enjoyed liberty and freedom, five, he was thankful to his God, and six, he was a strong and mighty man." Another question was, "If everyone was like Moroni, what would happen?" Brian answered: "The devil would not have power over the hearts of the children of men." His grade on the test was 86%.

In the middle of April, more than half way through the last term, we used another worksheet from the manual which included the following question: "This lesson has mentioned three very important gospel themes from 3 Nephi 17 and 18. You should have been pondering them. What do you think they are?" He answered, "One, pray often, two, keep the commandments, three, take the sacrament."

His change and progress was very exciting, but his behavior toward me had not changed. He still would not look at me. He still would not talk to me. His outward behavior was exactly the same. However, the things that he wrote and the things that I knew he was experiencing on the inside had changed dramatically. I don't know why. I like to think that some of the things I taught in seminary started to get through to him but I am convinced that it was the "power of the word" in the Book of Mormon that eventually penetrated his soul.

On another worksheet that included two pages of writing about what certain references mean and how they could be applied, he wrote, "If it weren't for the plan of redemption, as soon as they were dead, their souls would be miserable and cut off from the presence of the Lord." And, "It is expedient that mankind should be redeemed from spiritual death." Also, "Unless it were for repentance, mercy could not take effect, except it should destroy the work of justice." And, "All mankind were fallen and in the grasp of the justice of God." The last thing he wrote on that paper was: "Mercy cometh because of the atonement." His grade on that worksheet was 94%.

Brian finished the seminary year writing positive, knowledgeable, even wonderful, things. He never would look at me. He never did talk to me. There was no change on the outside. The year ended and he was no longer in my class.

Much later, I heard that he received a mission call. Before he left, there was an open house for his friends and family. I was not invited. Neither he, his parents, his bishop nor anybody else ever said anything to me about him. I was fine with that. In fact, I was thrilled with the way things turned out. It wasn't about me. How he felt about me really didn't matter. How he felt about the Lord did.

I'm not recommending that behavioral and classroom problems should always be handled the way I did that one. All I'm saying is that at that time it worked for me and more importantly, it worked for him.

We had a great teacher training session as we discussed that difficult student from so long ago. Numerous great insights were shared. I think that as a result of hearing this story and participating in the related discussion, many teachers were more prepared to deal with difficult students.

Discussion Questions

1. How can you use the things discussed in this chapter to help you deal with difficult people or situations?
2. Why do you think Brian changed?
3. What have you learned from this chapter that will help you to be a more confident and effective teacher?

CHAPTER 15
It Is Enough

"If thou art called to pass through tribulation; if thou art in perils among false brethren... If thou art accused with all manner of false accusations; if thine enemies fall upon thee... know thou, my son, that all these things shall give thee experience, and shall be for thy good. The Son of Man hath descended below them all. Art thou greater than he? Therefore, hold on thy way, and the priesthood shall remain with thee; for their bounds are set, they cannot pass. Thy days are known, and thy years shall not be numbered less; therefore, fear not what man can do, for God shall be with you forever and ever." (Doctrine and Covenants 122:5-9)

By the time I had been a teacher in the Church Educational System in three different locations for about 15 years I'd had many great experiences teaching seminary and institute. Most of my experiences had been very positive and I was quite happy and felt successful as a teacher. Generally speaking, I got along well with students, parents and priesthood leaders. I was feeling great about the many wonderful experiences I'd had in my profession.

We had spent six years in New Mexico and were hoping to get transferred back to Utah. However, I was asked by the Church Educational System to go to Fairview, Arizona and become the seminary principal. Later on, I was given the opportunity to teach some institute classes in that area. We had a difficult time finding a home and making the move. We were surprised that the president of the stake where the high school was located was quite upset that we considered buying a home outside of his stake boundaries. Eventually we managed to get our family settled and I started teaching at the seminary near the high school.

I didn't know that there had been problems with the students, parents, and priesthood leaders resulting in an unprecedented turnover of seminary teachers: four different teachers in five years. Classroom discipline was a bigger problem there than at any place I had taught before. There was no tradition of reverence or spirituality in seminary. Students used profanity and were involved in theft in the classroom. They were disrespectful towards each other and toward the teacher. When teaching seminary, the hope is that you're going to have spiritual experiences with your classes day after day, but in Fairview, that did not happen.

There were high bushes around the seminary. "Stoners" came over from the high school to hang out there, bringing drugs, drinking, smoking, and immorality. There seemed to be negativity and evil surrounding the seminary building.

It was not easy to get it approved, but we had a tall fence built all the way around the seminary. I also put up some motion alarms that would set off a siren and lights if people came sneaking around the seminary. First, they had a hard time getting over the fence and if they did get through, the alarms would go off. That solved most of the problems outside the seminary building. In the classroom, we had to have other kinds of fences and rules in order to get things under control. That was all difficult for me because I was not a "fences and rules" kind of teacher. But I had to change my style in order to be able to overcome the problems there.

I began keeping better track of attendance and tardies and established written goals for our classes and gave more writing assignments in order to have a more structured classroom environment. It didn't solve all the problems but we made significant progress. I also started a student leadership program that involved about thirty students in the seminary council and in classroom leadership. I did a lot of leadership training with the student leaders and it made a big difference. Classroom spirituality increased. Many good students began leading out in overcoming the negative traditions that had been established there.

One of the most outstanding leadership activities I was ever involved in took place during that time. We took all of the student leaders to a rugged and beautiful canyon that had a cold, clear creek flowing down it. There were many places where the creek went through and even under large rocks and there were many small waterfalls. Our family had previously had many great experiences there. We knew the place well and carefully planned and prepared for that leadership activity to be safe and meaningful. Our whole group of student leaders hiked on the trail, which was mostly above the river until we were about a mile up the canyon. Then we got down into the stream and followed it down.

We had a 200 foot rope and instructed them to hold on to the rope as if it were the iron rod described by Nephi. The idea was to be united in helping each other down the stream through all the rocks and waterfalls. By using the rope and helping each other, we were all able to make it over, around, and through many potentially dangerous places without injury. It was adventurous, challenging, and required continuous teamwork.

About halfway down, we had to get down a waterfall that was about twelve feet high with a large waist-deep pool at the bottom. The course of study that year was New Testament. After we all helped each other down, I gave them a lesson about Christ being the Rock of our salvation. I also taught them about Peter being a leader chosen by Christ, and that Christ actually gave him the name of Peter, which means rock. I explained to them that they were called to be leaders for Christ, and that they should also be rocks of discipleship and good leadership, like Peter turned out to be.

Before we got to that waterfall, my son, Mike, slipped away from the group according to plan and hid in a crevice with an air pocket behind the waterfall, holding a bag of beautiful rocks. After the lesson, I asked them to watch carefully. I went into the waterfall to where Mike was courageously hiding. He handed me one of the rocks. In less than a minute, I emerged from the waterfall holding a beautiful rock. All the students were completely surprised. I showed them the rock and explained that it represented Christ and Peter and me. I told them that there were more rocks behind the waterfall representing Christ and Peter and each one of them. I explained that each of them needed to go through the waterfall alone in order to get their very own rock.

They had lots of questions, but I told them that they just needed to have faith and they would be able to get their own rock. I did not tell them about Mike hidden back there with the rocks. There was a lot of water and force in the waterfall, so it was not easy to get through. Many of them were afraid. However, a few were excited to make the attempt. As each one made it through, Mike handed them their rock and instructed them not to tell the others about him or how they got it. As each one emerged with their rock, excitement and courage grew until everyone developed more faith than fear, and got their rock. Finally, a very cold Mike came out of the waterfall.

We had a group hug with some tears of gratitude, faith, love, and commitment.

While we were making significant progress with most, there was still a minority of the students who consistently fought against any improvement. They were not interested in spiritual things and they wanted to be in control. Efforts were made to get parents and priesthood leaders involved to try to solve the problems, but I soon realized that there were some parents and priesthood leaders who were not supportive. They seemed to believe that if there was any kind of a problem, it couldn't be the students' fault, the teacher just needed to do better.

One student came ten to fifteen minutes late to class nearly every day. I called his parents and asked them to meet with me to discuss this problem. When they came to the meeting, I took out the roll and showed them that he had been late to seventeen out of twenty classes. I hoped that we could work together to resolve that problem.

The parents were adamant, "Our son doesn't have a problem."

I was surprised. "What do you mean, he doesn't have a problem?"

"It's not his problem. It's your problem. If you were a good enough teacher, he would want to be here and he'd want to be here on time."

I disagreed. "It's not just your son's problem, it's your problem! Until you have the right attitude about this, it's going to be very difficult for your son to make any progress in life."

They became angry with me, so I suggested that we check with all his other teachers in order to verify the source of the problem. They knew he had a long history of tardiness and behavioral problems, which they had consistently blamed on teachers. I explained that if they wanted their son to be successful in life, they needed to quit enabling his misbehavior. They were not happy, but after that his attendance improved.

After that meeting, I contacted their Bishop, but he was no help at all. Sadly, there were a significant number of students, parents, and priesthood leaders in that area who had attitudes similar to those of this student and his parents. There was gradual improvement, but it was much slower progress than it needed to be.

I was there for a total of three years. Things improved quite a bit the first year. The second year and the third year, things were getting even better. However, there was a group of students, parents, and priesthood leaders who did not recognize the progress and were not supportive. It became very clear why previous teachers were forced out.

At some point during the time I was there, a group of students decided that they didn't like the discipline and spirituality. I suspected it at the time, and found out years later that it was true that they formed a secret group, committed to disrupting the seminary and to getting rid of me. I don't know how many people were in this group or exactly how they were organized. Their tactics eventually became obvious.

We had a seminary activity one night and several students brought a local drug addict to disrupt what we were doing. I treated him kindly, but explained to him that this activity was only for seminary students, and that it would be necessary for him to leave. For a little while I thought we might have to call the police, but he eventually left without causing a major disruption. The students who brought him and encouraged him to stay were bothered when he left, and they left soon thereafter.

One particular student, Jim Tanner, was a constant problem and disruption. Several times, I had to take him into my office to talk with him. "Jim, if you're going to remain in seminary you need to stop disrupting the class. Most of the other students are trying to have positive spiritual experiences here. We can't allow you to ruin it."

Each time he would respond, "I'll try to do better," and then he would continue to behave poorly. The funny thing was, I kind of liked Jim. I felt like he had potential and I really wanted to help him, so I always spoke with him kindly, but also firmly. He had a negative effect, but we managed to get through the year with him in my class.

The next year, I had a student teacher who came and taught three additional classes in the room next to mine. Jim was in one of those classes. He was the source of almost constant disruption and discipline problems in that class. The student teacher had the potential to become a good full-time seminary teacher. However, due to disruption led by Jim, he gave up on being a teacher after a few months. It was a sad thing. We appointed a part-time teacher, Sister Griggs. She was a wonderful woman, had a great family, and was a good teacher.

When she started teaching, I took Jim into my office and told him that I wasn't his teacher, but I was the seminary principal. I explained to him that his disruptions had contributed substantially to the loss of the student teacher. I explained to him that we had a new teacher and that for the sake of the students and the new teacher, the class had to stay under control. I told him that he had to become less disruptive or he would have to be removed from seminary. I explained to him that I wanted him to have a positive experience in seminary and that I wanted him to understand and appreciate spiritual things but that if he continued to be disruptive he would lose the privilege of attending seminary.

I had tried to talk to his parents and his bishop and there was no support from them to help stop his misbehavior. He went back into the class and his attitude and actions remained the same. It was almost impossible for Sister Griggs to teach the class, let alone for them to have any spiritual experiences. Jim was the ringleader of all the class problems. It wasn't long until I called him into my office. "Jim, I'm sorry but it's like I explained to you. You can't stay in seminary and be disruptive." I handed him a paper saying that he had lost his privilege to attend seminary and told him that he would have to go back over to the high school and tell them that he couldn't attend seminary any more.

He seemed surprised. "What am I supposed to do? What class am I going to go to? What's going to happen?"

"I don't know. When you were here at the seminary, it was my responsibility, but what happens with the school is up to you and them. I will continue to care about you and your life, but you have chosen to proceed without seminary."

After he was gone, that class immediately got a lot better. I guess part of it was just not having him there, and another part of it was the kids realizing that the same thing could happen to them. They did not want to get kicked out of seminary. I spoke with Sister Griggs' class about the importance of being supportive of her in order to have a good atmosphere in seminary. I did all I could to help her and to help the other students, and they ended up having a great seminary experience.

Seminary dances that were held during the year were part of my responsibility. One particular dance was well-attended and the kids were having a really good time. Sister Griggs and I were the chaperones. The music and dancing were appropriate, and the dance was a good, wholesome, fun activity.

Attending the dance were two young men who were part of the "secret combination." They would wait on the side until some students were dancing in front of them and then they would run out on the floor and dive into or tackle the dancers, knocking them down, hoping to disrupt the dance. Then they got up, laughing and smirking, and went back to sit on the side again. I saw this happen a couple of times and I could see that it was dangerous.

I knew that it had to be stopped. I walked out on the dance floor as they were getting up. I took each of them by an arm in a firm but not hurtful grip and said, "Please come with me." Then I walked them off the dance floor and out into the hall. The music and dance continued. "What you were doing is dangerous. People could get hurt and we can't have that going on here at the dance. You'll need to leave and not return tonight."

When we got close to the exit, I let go of their arms. One of them whirled around and hit me in the face. He was not a very big kid, but I think he hit me as hard as he could. It hurt. He was expecting me to hit him back but I didn't. I just looked at him. "That's it. You need to leave now!" He and his friend looked at each other and then turned and ran out the door.

Outside, they were joined by about ten more rough characters. They screamed threats and obscenities about me, about the seminary, and about the church. Some of the other students saw them and heard what they were saying. Several of our student leaders said something like, "We should go out and make those guys go away. They shouldn't be able to do this."

I stopped them. "No. Don't go out there. If they come back in the building, I will call the police. Otherwise, let's just stay in here and you guys go and have fun at the dance." When the crowd outside saw that we weren't paying any attention to them, they dispersed. The good kids went back into the dance and we finished up the evening without additional problems.

I knew that what had happened at the dance was serious so I went home and wrote down a description, including the names of those involved. The next afternoon, I met with the stake president to discuss the events. He had already heard from the boys and their parents. They had told him that they were just minding their own business at the dance, when I physically threw them out and punched one of them without provocation. The stake president told me I was in deep trouble.

I protested. "That is entirely false. It happened exactly as I wrote it up."

He didn't listen. "I'm going to talk with your supervisors in the Church Educational System and arrange to have you removed from your position. I've received statements from these people. I've prayed about it and I know from the statements and from my own spiritual confirmation that they are telling me the truth and that you are lying. It's time for you to confess exactly what happened."

"President, I already told you."

"But I told you, the Spirit told me that what you said was a lie."

"Well President, you must be listening to the wrong spirit."

He yelled at me, "How dare you? How dare you tell me that I'm listening to the wrong spirit."

"Do you want me to tell you how I dare do that?"

"Yes, I do." His face was an angry red.

"Here's how I dare do it. I was there. I was there! I experienced it and I know the truth."

He continued to accuse me of lying and eventually dismissed me from his office. He told me that he would be in touch with my superiors, that I would be fired from my job and that there was a possibility of church disciplinary action against me.

I left and went home in shock. My integrity, my professional standing, and my membership in the church were in question as a result of false accusations. I told my wife. She was devastated. We didn't know what to do or what to think.

I taught seminary the next day amid rumors that something terrible had happened, and that I was going to get fired. I did the best I could to teach my classes and not discuss anything. A majority of the students and parents supported me and were concerned. They knew that the things being said weren't true. A minority of students, parents and leaders had bought into the lies, and they were much more vocal and demanding. The stake president called a meeting and asked for a representative from the Church Educational System to attend. I asked just one set of parents who were supportive of me, and their son, who had attended the dance, to come to the meeting. I explained the whole situation to them and asked them if they would be there to represent the majority of the parents and students.

Prior to the meeting, I fasted and prayed and asked the stake president for a second opportunity to talk with him. I went in and knelt and prayed with him, asking that he be guided and that we could have the Spirit with us. I was quite hopeful, but the second meeting went no better than the first. The stake president was adamant that my guilt was confirmed by his spiritual discernment. He seemed to be unaware of the following rule established by the Prophet Joseph Smith:

> A woman…began to accuse another sister of things that she was not guilty of, which she said she knew was so by the Spirit, but was afterwards proven to be false; she placed herself in the capacity of the "accuser of the brethren," and no person through the discerning of spirits can bring a charge against another, they must be proven guilty by positive evidence, or they stand clear. (*History of the Church*, 4:581)

Not too long before the big meeting, a somewhat shy young man who was a seminary student came to my office. "I need to talk to you in private. You know that night at the dance when the trouble happened? You didn't see me and neither did the other boys, but I had just come out of the restroom and I was in the hall behind you. I saw and heard what happened."

I could have jumped for joy. "That's great! Can you tell me what you saw and heard?"

"Yes!" He told me exactly what happened as I knew it had happened. He had seen the kid hit me and that I didn't hit him back.

"This is wonderful. Your witness and testimony is very important. A lot rides on it. Are you willing to stand by this?"

"Yes I am."

We worked together to write down his account of what he saw and he signed it. He was concerned about what might happen if the other students found out that he was the witness, and even afraid for his safety. He said, "I was afraid to come forward, but I felt like I had to. I hope you can handle this so that they don't find out who I am."

"If I can do that, I will. I'll tell the stake president that we have a witness and that you are willing to come forward and talk with him, but that you would prefer to remain anonymous to the other kids if possible."

"That would be great."

I was so grateful for that young man. I made copies of his statement. It was just a few days before the meeting.

When we went to the meeting, the stake president was out of town on business, but his two counselors were there. The first counselor was conducting the meeting. In the high council room there were people sitting all around the table, and more in the chairs around the room. I was sitting at the right end of the table. The counselor said, "We want to get to the bottom of this matter in this meeting. Brother Van Shaar and his wife are here along with various students and parents. We have a representative from the Church Educational System here with us so that he can hear and document what is said and then report back to the administration. Let's start over here on the left side of the table and go around and let everyone in turn say whatever they want to about this situation." The statements began and there were students and parents who said that I had hit the boy and that I had done other inappropriate things. It went on and on.

Finally it got around to the good, strong young man who was a student leader, there to represent the majority of the students. Sadly, by the time it got to him, he was very angry and emotional about the lies and horrible things that had been said. He was red and shaking and so distraught that he had difficulty speaking, lost control, and had to leave the room.

I felt very bad for him. The stress of hearing such inaccuracies about me and about the incident at the dance was more than he could handle. Then his mother and father spoke up. They said, "Our son is upset, but we know how he feels and what he knows." They spoke up very strongly in my behalf. They said that the things the other students and parents had said were not true. They said they were speaking for most of the students and parents, and that they were appalled by the lies that had been presented as truth in the meeting. They said that those who had said those things should know better and should be ashamed. They spoke up for me wonderfully, and I was very grateful.

The first counselor then said, "Brother Van Shaar, do you have anything to say for yourself. Even though these people have spoken up for you, we have all these other witnesses against you and the evidence is quite damning." The person who was there representing the administration of the Church Educational System later told me that at that point he figured it was all over. He said he didn't believe any of the allegations against me, and that he was on my side, but with that many students, parents, and the stake presidency against me, he just figured I was going to lose my job.

When it was my turn to speak I said, "Before I make my statement, I need to inform you that an eyewitness has come forward. That witness is not here, but he was there and saw what happened at the dance. He is prepared to make himself known to the stake presidency. He is worried about the possible reaction of some of the students involved, but he is willing to affirm his written statement privately to the stake presidency. I would like to read you his statement." Then I read his statement, which contradicted the things the other people had said. It told how the kid had hit me but I didn't hit him, and everything else right down the line as I had reported it.

I then affirmed that I had told the truth, that I had behaved appropriately, that there was now an additional witness to prove it, and that I would not back down. Then I became the first and only one in the meeting to bear my testimony and end all I had said in the name of Jesus Christ. I felt that I had spoken with the power of the Spirit. I was very thankful for the student who came forward, and for the Lord's help.

It was quiet for a minute. Then the first counselor stood and said, "I think that everybody involved should say they are sorry and we should just forget this whole thing. We are not going to take any action. We are going to end this meeting now." The room cleared out quickly, including the first counselor. Nobody apologized.

After my wife and I got outside, the second counselor in the stake presidency came up to us. "I couldn't say much in the meeting because I'm only the second counselor. I know how the stake president and the first counselor felt and how those other parents felt, but I want you to know that I know that what you told us is true and that all of this was wrong."

I said, "I'm very grateful that you feel that way. What are you going to do about it?"

He said, "I can't really do anything. I just want you to know how I feel."

That was the closest anyone came to apologizing. Most of the other seminary students and their parents didn't know much about the meeting, but some of them became aware of what had happened and expressed their support for me. Among those were two former stake presidents who told me how upset they were about how things had been going in the seminary for years. They said they were grateful for all I had done to clean up the seminary problems.

Teaching seminary the last few months of that year was fairly difficult because the kids who had been involved in the conspiracy had not been held accountable, nor had they repented. They would smugly come to class and sometimes make things difficult, but were careful not to go too far. I just did the best I could to be a good teacher, to be loving and kind, and to have the Spirit in the classroom. It was certainly better than it was when I had first arrived there, but it was not as good as it could have been.

After all of this happened, I did a lot of thinking and praying because I was concerned about what kind of attitude I should have about it. I understood that sometimes people were persecuted for the truth. I had always thought, "Okay, I've got a strong enough testimony and I'm well enough founded that no matter what persecution happens, I'll stand up to it and I'll be true and strong." But I was having a much harder time than I expected.

There were even a few times when I didn't feel like going to church. That had never happened before. I thought about it and asked myself, "What is going on here?" Then I thought, "You know what? I always figured that if there was persecution, that it would come from the outside. I didn't think it would come from within the church, especially from church leaders."

I spent quite a bit of time out in a wilderness area by the river, kneeling in the sand and praying. I asked the Lord, "Why did this happen? What should I learn from it? Where do I go from here?" I wasn't demanding, but I was seeking understanding. I had some very powerful and distinct thoughts come into my mind. I recognized that they were coming from the Lord. It was more than a feeling. These words came to my mind: "It was necessary for you to be tried, even as others of my servants, including Abraham, had to be tried." When the voice said that, I understood. I knew that I wasn't tested on the level that Abraham was, but for me it was a very severe, difficult test. I received the witness that it was an Abrahamic test. I then understood what had happened and that I had passed the test. I cried and expressed my gratitude to the Lord for his help and comfort, and I renewed my commitment to him and his church.

Not long after that, one of the administrators in the Church Educational System called me and offered me an institute position that was a definite advancement in my career. It wasn't, however, in Utah, and we wanted to go back to Utah. It was in Missouri, which was farther away. I was concerned about not continuing the battle in Fairview. I knew I was fighting in the trenches on the Lord's side, and that I had been wounded but was undefeated. I felt like I had a responsibility to stay there and make sure no other teacher would have to face the things I had. I wanted to finalize the positive changes that had been made there. Therefore, I told the administrator that I was very interested in the assignment, but I was not sure about what to do. He told me he wanted me to pray about it over the weekend and then call him back with my decision on Monday. I went back out to that same spot on the edge of the desert near the river and I prayed about whether or not I should accept that new position. It did not take long for the Lord to clearly say, "**It is enough.** There are things for you to do and blessings in store for you in other places. Accept the position." I called the administrator back on Monday and told him that the Lord had inspired me to accept the position. He said, "I knew that's what would happen. I already had a witness that you should go to Missouri."

We arranged to go to our new assignment in June. Near the end of the school year, we had stake seminary graduation under the direction of the stake president. In his talk, the stake president said, "We would like to express appreciation to Brother Van Shaar. We know that he is a man of God." He said a few other positive things about the seminary program. He never did say anything else to me about any of the issues we'd had.

We were transferred to Missouri. From the very beginning, it was a wonderful experience with the students, parents, and priesthood leaders, and especially with the stake presidency, whom I worked with closely. We hadn't been there very long when the stake president called me to serve on the high council. After I had been there a few months, the stake president wrote a letter about me to the CES administration. He read the letter to me, which said, among other things, "Brother Van Shaar is a breath of fresh air" and that they were thankful to have me there as the director of the institute and supervisor of seminary programs. I had experienced those kinds of things before, but it was wonderful to be back in a supportive environment.

About two years later, we were at home there in Missouri when there was a knock at the door. I opened the door to find two missionaries standing there. I was shocked to see that one of them was Jim Tanner. I invited them to come in and sit down in the living room. Barbra and I sat across the room from them.

Jim looked uncomfortable. "I have been assigned by the mission president to work in this area, specifically at the at the institute. I told the mission president that I would only be able to do that if I received your permission. Would you be willing to listen to my story?"

I was curious. "Of course."

"When I was in seminary, I thought it was all foolishness. I didn't understand spiritual things. I didn't believe in them. I had never prayed or read the scriptures. I thought it was all dumb. Even though many people denied its existence, I was part of the group that made secret plans to get rid of you. We agreed that we would protect each other and that we would do whatever we had to: lie, scheme, set traps, anything."

I was not surprised. I had suspected that such a group existed, but his confession was the first time anyone had actually told me about it. His description met the scriptural definition of a secret combination.

Jim said he was shocked when I removed him from seminary. After he was expelled from seminary, his opportunity for influence was very limited compared to those in the group who remained in seminary. "I need to tell you what happened to me after that. The next year I went to Fairview College. I noticed that a lot of students there often went to the institute building. I wandered into the institute and there were a lot of fun things going on. There were also a lot of kids talking about how great the classes were. I thought about how I'd been kicked out of seminary but I hadn't been kicked out of institute. I decided to go to an institute class just to show that I could."

He quickly observed that it was not like a high school class. Nobody was acting up or speaking out of turn. He quickly realized that if he said or did anything negative in institute, the other students would look down on him, so he just sat there and listened. Then he went back to the next class and sat and listened. The teacher and many of the students were saying things that were very interesting and made him feel good. He kept going and kept listening. Before long, he started going to another institute class, and then another. Eventually, he was listening and learning in three concurrent institute classes.

He said that he started to think more, to pray and read the scriptures, and to repent. By the end of that year, his whole life had changed. He decided that he wanted to go on a mission, so he went and talked to his bishop. There was a waiting period, but eventually he got clearance and was called to serve in a mission that covered our part of Missouri.

Jim said, "I've tried to be a good missionary. I've been in the mission field about a year, and during that time I have read the entire Book of Mormon seven times. I work so hard that I wear out my companions. I want to be a good missionary in this area at the institute, but if you don't want me here, I will tell the mission president that I have to be transferred somewhere else. I want you to know I'm very, very sorry about everything I did against the seminary and you. I've repented for it over and over again, and I want to stay here." He looked up at me with tears in his eyes and asked, "Will you forgive me?"

I stood up and walked across the room. He stood up and we looked each other in the eyes. I cried and I put my arms around him. "Yes, I will!" We stood there and hugged and cried for quite a while. It was a healing moment for him, and for me.

I had passed beyond those experiences in Fairview. They were behind me, but I was not healed until I stood there hugging and crying with Jim. The Spirit was very strong and we were both comforted.

Jim stayed there and worked as a missionary at the institute. He worked hard and was an outstanding missionary. He and I became very good friends. We worked together in the Lord's work for about four months, teaching investigators and helping people get baptized. It was a great time for us both. When it came time for him to leave, I was sorry that he had to go, but I was grateful that he had come.

It was clearly not a coincidence that he was called to serve there. Of all the places in the world he could have gone, he was sent to where I was so that we could be healed together. What a wonderful experience that was, and how grateful I was for Jim.

I don't know what happened to most of the other people from Fairview, but the first counselor in the stake presidency was called on a mission to Adam-ondi-Ahman in Missouri. I was taking a group of institute students to Adam-ondi-Ahman on a field trip. I contacted the Adam-ondi-Ahman missionaries to make arrangements and was surprised that he was my assigned contact. We were very polite with each other. We talked several times. The field trip turned out well. However, he avoided saying anything about the Fairview events.

About fourteen years later, I was visiting the Fairview area for a wedding. The former second counselor in the stake presidency was there. At the time of the wedding he was the stake president. He and I made a point to sit at the same table. We talked about some of the things that had happened. He told me how bad he felt about what had happened and that he was unable to help more. I told him about my experience in Missouri with Jim. We cried and rejoiced together.

At that same wedding, I was surprised when a parent of one of my former seminary students there approached me and said that as a student her daughter did not like me much. I smiled and said, "Ah, but I always loved her, and isn't she wonderful?"

The Fairview experience was one of the most difficult times of my life. It was also one of my greatest times of learning. It was hard to stay there, but then also hard to leave. It has been a source of comfort to me to know that what I gave there in service to the Lord and to the seminary students was "enough."

Discussion Questions

1. What did you learn from the leadership activity at the waterfall?
2. How were some of the students, parents, and priesthood leaders in this chapter different than most you have known?
3. What would you have done differently if you were the stake president?
4. What can you learn from this chapter about how to deal with persecution and/or Abrahamic tests?
5. What did you learn from Jim Tanner?

CHAPTER 16
Something Worse Than Lonely

"And now these three remain: faith, hope and love. But the greatest of these is love." (NIV I Corinthians 13:13; Moroni 7:47).

When I was serving as a bishop in Missouri, a young woman in her mid-twenties came in to speak to me. She had been married and divorced three times, which is unusual for someone so young. She was active in the church and seemed to be doing the best she could to live the Gospel. She was an attractive person, but it was obvious that she was lonely. I wanted to encourage her and help her feel better. I said something along the line of, "It must be difficult sometimes to be alone."

"There's something that's a lot more difficult and much more sad than being alone," she replied.

"And what is that?"

She looked at me and said, very earnestly, "The worst thing of all is being married to someone you don't love, or who doesn't love you."

This declaration struck me hard. It was so profound. I wished that I could have had every one of the young women and young men in our ward talk to this sister. I wished I could help all of them understand how important it is to marry someone who is willing to live the gospel, to find someone who loves and treasures you as you do them, and not settle for someone who is less than you deserve.

This sister and I went on talking. Even though she was fairly young, she had learned some hard lessons from her failed marriages. She had no intention of making those mistakes again. Earlier in her life, she was afraid of being alone and had settled for company that was not worthy of her. Life had taught her that being alone was not the worst thing. You never feel more alone than when you are sharing space with someone who doesn't truly care about you, isn't there for you, who refuses to understand you, someone you do not love or who doesn't love you in return. Being alone can never equal the intensity of that loneliness. This young woman learned that lesson the hard way. She was determined that she would never make that mistake again. I know she spoke the truth, and I hope that others can learn from this short, simple, and profound lesson that she taught me.

Discussion Questions

1. What are the most important things to consider when choosing a spouse?
2. How can you develop the faith, hope, and courage to keep searching for true love?
3. If you are in a loveless marriage, what are your best options?

CHAPTER 17
Call from Jail

"Draw near unto me and I will draw near unto you; seek me dili-gently and ye shall find me; ask, and ye shall receive; knock, and it shall be opened unto you." (D&C 88:63)

While serving as Bishop I had an unusual experience during one of our Wednesday evening bishopric meetings. We had opened our meeting with prayer and were discussing ward business when we were interrupted by a phone call from a sister who lived in our ward whom we had never met.

Jane urgently explained that she was in the county jail for writing bad checks. Her husband had forced her to write the checks in order to support his drug habit. She knew that what she had done was wrong. She was very distressed and needed our help. She did not know how long she would be in jail. She was worried that her two young children were home with her husband who was under the influence of drugs. It was a cold winter and they had neither electricity nor heat. The utilities had been turned off in their house because the bill had not been paid. There was nothing she could do about it from jail and she didn't know who else to call for help. She begged us to do something to keep her children safe. Unfortunately, if the police got involved, there was a good chance that the husband would be arrested on drug charges and the children would be taken into the custody of child protective services. With both parents in jail, she could lose custody of her children, and she couldn't bear to have that happen. She wanted us to know that she was a good mother who took good care of her children and that she was going to do everything she could to keep the children safe. She pleaded for us to do something to help her children. Matters were further complicated by the presence of weapons in the house. She considered her husband to be dangerous when on drugs. She told us she was not going to be allowed to make another telephone call and that we would be the only ones who could help her children.

Naturally, all other matters were set aside and we focused the meeting on considering how best to aid Jane and her children. We all felt overwhelmed. We discussed the situation and sought to make a decision on how to respond. I certainly never expected that in my calling as a bishop I would need to make decisions that could affect families in such a profound way. It was potentially a life or death decision. After much discussion, none of us could come up with a solution to this dilemma. Turning our hearts and minds to the Lord, we knelt and prayed together. We asked the Lord to guide us and help us find a way to help this woman and her children. After pleading with the Lord in faith, we sat back down and once again considered our options.

Could we go to the apartment or send somebody from our ward to see if we could assist? There was no way to know what the man would do. With drugs and weapons at the scene, this seemed too risky to attempt. We didn't know if he would be receptive to letting us help take care of his children. We didn't know if he would be violent. We were concerned that we might do more harm than good.

What if we notified the police? This seemed like the right thing to do, but Jane had specifically pleaded with us not to do so. It felt like betrayal to respond to her plea for help by doing something that could cause her to lose custody of her children. We discussed several other possibilities, but there was nothing we felt comfortable with.

We worked on this problem for about an hour and it was starting to get late. We felt pressure to do something, but were still unable to arrive at a decision. We decided to pray again. We knelt down, all three of us taking turns to pray out loud and plead for the Lord's help and guidance in this difficult situation.

When we finished our prayer, we again discussed the problem and were still drawing a blank. We felt desperate. At that point, every option we could think of had been thoroughly considered and discarded. Then I felt a sudden and very strong impression that I should call the chief of police in the small city where the family lived and explain the situation to him. I explained this impression to the others. We agreed to make the call.

It was about 8:30 p.m. when I called the police station and explained that I had an urgent matter that I needed to discuss with the police chief. It only took a few minutes for the chief to come on the line with me. He introduced himself and asked what he could do to help. I explained that I was the bishop of a local congregation of the Church of Jesus Christ of Latter-day Saints and had an urgent problem to discuss with him. I explained the whole situation to him, giving the names and address. I asked if there was anything that he could do to help, and if there was some way that the custody of the children could be protected until the mother was released from jail.

He immediately asked, "Do you have anyone in your congregation who can take care of these children?"

My counselors and I had already discussed that. There was a family in the ward that we trusted who knew Jane's family and had occasionally tended the children. I told the police chief that we did have someone in the congregation who would take care of the children.

"Okay," he said. "Here's what we're going to do. I will send officers out to investigate. If there is evidence of drug abuse, we'll take the man into custody and bring the children in to the police station. If that happens I will call you, and you will need to get someone here very quickly to take the children. Can you do that?" I said we could and that we would be waiting for his call.

I called the couple in our ward, explained the situation, and asked if they would be willing to help. They said they knew and loved the children and would willingly do what was needed. They agreed to go pick up the children, take them home, and care for them until the mother was released from jail. We thanked them very much and asked them to wait for our call.

About an hour later, the police chief called and reported that officers had been out to the residence. There were obvious drug violations and they had taken the man into custody. The children were at the police station. They were upset and we needed to get our people there quickly. I thanked him for his help and assured him that our people would be there in a few minutes. He told me that they appreciated our involvement and willingness to help.

We called the couple in our ward and asked them to hurry to the police station. It was not long before they called us back and told us they had the children in their home. They added that the children were comfortable and happy to be where they had warmth and food. I expressed great appreciation to them.

We had no way of getting word to their mother in jail unless someone actually went to visit her. I asked my wife Barbra if she would be willing to go and meet with Jane, explain what had happened, and assure her that her children were being well cared for. Barbra was able to do so, and Jane was very relieved and happy with the outcome.

Less than a week later, Jane was released from jail and quickly made arrangements to take the custody of her children and move to a safe location. Her husband was incarcerated for some time and she eventually left the area. We later heard that things turned out well for the mother and the children.

My counselors and I were very thankful that the Lord had inspired us and helped us. We were amazed at how cooperative the police chief had been and at how well things had turned out when there was potential for so much trouble. We felt like we had been inspired and we felt blessed. We were very thankful for the family in our ward who took care of the children. We felt like the Lord hadn't just heard our prayers, but also heard and answered the prayers of that frantic mother.

Many times since then I've reflected on the idea that there is no way to predict when unusual circumstances will arise that can involve life and death decisions. This can be a heavy burden on leaders, but we can be assured that when we are in the service of the Lord and our fellow men, and if we are spiritually prepared, the Lord will help us to bear the responsibility so that we can serve as needed. When we have hard decisions to make, the answer is not always obvious. The Lord expects us to think, ponder, and stretch our abilities. Then if there is a need he will step in and give us additional inspiration. He hears and answers prayers, including the desperate pleas of a mother in jail.

Discussion Questions

1. How could something like what happened to Jane happen to you or someone you love?
2. Since Jane was less active in the church, why did she call the Bishop?
3. How do you feel about the police chief?
4. How are you similar to the ward members who took in the children?
5. If you are ever involved in a desperate situation how will you handle it?

CHAPTER 18
Forgiven

"For they shall all know me, from the least of them unto the greatest of them, saith the Lord: for I will forgive their iniquity, and I will remember their sin no more." (Jeremiah 31:34)

When I was a bishop, a woman made an appointment to see me. She was fairly new in the ward and it was the first time I had talked with her. Not long into our visit, she started a lengthy confession of many serious transgressions.

After we talked for a while, I asked her why she was coming to see me after being away from the church for many years. She responded, "I need to go to the temple with my children."

"We have discussed some very serious things, and it will take some time to work through this."

She answered with resolve, "I understand that. But I want to do whatever I have to do for as long as it takes. I need to go to the temple with my children."

Many years earlier, she had been married to a man who was eventually called to be a stake president. She felt that he was a good stake president who performed in that office well. However, he encouraged her to start drinking alcoholic beverages in order to help relax her inhibitions and promote more intimacy. Some people seem to be more susceptible to alcoholism than others and it turned out that she was one of those people. Once she started drinking, it was very difficult for her to control it.

I asked her how she felt about him serving as the stake president when something so obviously inappropriate was going on. She answered, "I know that what he did with me was wrong, but as far as I know, in every other way, he was a good stake president." In many ways he was a good husband but they did have some serious problems. Eventually, her husband was released from being the stake president and they were divorced.

After the divorce, he drifted away from the church. She also stopped attending church and continued to drink. She was involved in various kinds of immorality over a period of many years. The things she confessed were very serious and seemed to necessitate excommunication, especially considering that she had previously held responsible callings, and had violated temple covenants.

After meeting with her several times, I discussed the situation with the stake president. He and I both agreed that it would be necessary to hold a bishop's disciplinary council which would probably result in excommunication, and hopefully lead to re-baptism. I scheduled a disciplinary council for her. In the meantime, I continued to counsel with her. She was almost to the point of complete abstinence with her drinking. She really worked hard to get her life cleaned up.

The afternoon of the disciplinary council arrived. As bishop, I presided in the council, which included my two counselors and a clerk. After I briefed my counselors, she was invited into the meeting. I had previously instructed her to avoid giving unnecessary or embarrassing details. The sister made a brief but honest confession. She was very emotional and sincerely stated that she wanted to be forgiven. It was clear that she understood that she would probably need to be excommunicated. She affirmed that she would do whatever was necessary to be re-baptized and receive a restoration of blessings. Her greatest desire was to be completely forgiven and be able to go to the temple with her children.

We excused her from the room so that we could discuss things as a bishopric and come to a decision. It seemed fairly obvious that the decision would need to be excommunication. We knelt in prayer and asked the Lord to guide us. When we finished the prayer we all sat back down. I was surprised that I had no feeling of confirmation about excommunication. I asked my first counselor to express his feelings. He said that it was obvious that she needed to be excommunicated so that she could be completely forgiven and brought back into the church. My second counselor's opinion was different. He said that he had a strong impression that she should not be excommunicated, but only disfellowshipped.

The first counselor was incredulous. He couldn't believe it. "Did you hear what she's done? It's obvious that she should be excommunicated!"

The second counselor disagreed. "I really feel strongly that she should only be disfellowshipped, not excommunicated."

So they discussed the issue back and forth for a while. Finally, one of them turned to me, "Bishop, how do you feel?"

I was still unclear about what should be done. "I don't know. Let's pray about it again."

We knelt again and this time each of us took a turn praying out loud. Once again, I got absolutely nothing. I was drawing a complete blank. My first counselor said that after praying about it the second time, he was even more convinced that she needed to be excommunicated. The second counselor said that this time, he was even more convinced that she should only be disfellowshipped. They were in complete disagreement. Both of them turned to me and told me that as the bishop, it was my job to sort it out and reach an inspired decision. I responded, "I'm sorry, brethren, but I just don't know."

On the wall in the bishop's office, I had a plaque based on a favorite quote by Brigham Young. Its application was very important in my life and ministry. It says,

> If you would always pause and say, I have no counsel for you, I have no answer for you on this subject, because I have no manifestation of the Spirit, and be willing to let everybody in the world know that you are ignorant when you are, you would become wise a great deal quicker than to give counsel on your own judgment, without the Spirit of revelation. (GVS, *The Best of Joseph and Brigham*, 116)

I was the director of the Institute of Religion as well as the bishop of the ward, and many people expected me to know everything. However, it was my experience that many times I did not know what the Lord's will was, or exactly what should or should not be done. There were times when the Spirit was very clear and it was easy to give counsel that I knew came from the Lord. But there were also times when, as Brigham said, there was "no manifestation of the Spirit." I made up my mind that I was going to try to follow Brigham's counsel because I didn't want to be responsible for telling somebody the wrong thing and having them believe it was from the Lord. Therefore, it was very important to me to seek revelation but be willing to admit when I had not received it. Sometimes, the best I could do was to encourage people to continue to seek the answers for themselves.

That plaque was there on the wall and we were in that situation where I didn't feel like I could decide because I had not had a confirmation of the Spirit one way or the other. It was very difficult because I had counselors whose opinions were diametrically opposed. My answer had to be, "I don't know."

My counselors were very frustrated. One of them said, "You know that we are not going to come to an agreement here. As the presiding officer you need to make the final decision, and it needs to be inspired."

"Well, brethren, I'm sorry, but I don't know."

We continued to talk back and forth for a while. The situation was a difficult one and there was tension in the room. I suggested that we kneel again and each pray silently. I felt we should continue to pray that way until we got the answers we needed. We did that for more than ten minutes and I continued to get nothing. There was no confirmation either way.

Then all of a sudden, the first counselor jumped up from the floor so fast that his chair tipped over backwards and hit the wall. He was the one who had been so adamant that the sister should be excommunicated. He exclaimed, "Bishop! She's not supposed to be excommunicated!"

The other counselor jumped up. "That's what I've been trying to tell you!"

The first one replied, "I thought it was obvious that she should be, but the Spirit just clearly told me that she should not."

At that moment, one of the strongest spiritual impressions that I've ever had in my life came to me, along with a flood of intelligence. It was so powerful that it was almost overwhelming. I knew, absolutely, that this sister was not supposed to be excommunicated and I knew why. I told the brethren that I had received revelation and knew exactly what we were supposed to do and asked if they were prepared to support it. They had also felt the power of the Spirit and responded in the affirmative.

We invited the sister back into the office and she sat down. I announced the decision. "Sister, after prayerful consideration, we have decided that you are to be disfellowshipped."

Startled, she began to cry. "That can't be right."

"Why not?"

"I know how serious the things are that I've done. I know the rules of the Church and I think I have to be excommunicated in order to wipe the slate clean."

I smiled. "The Lord revealed to us that the decision to disfellowship is right. He also revealed to me why it is right. He told me that most of the responsibility for what happened to you belongs to your former husband. You have some responsibility, but much of it is upon him. The Lord told me, in no uncertain terms, that if it wouldn't have been for your husband's position in the church, and his influence on you, you never would have started drinking, never would have fallen away from the Church, and never would have been involved in those serious sins. Your former husband can also repent and be forgiven, but that is a separate issue. Therefore, we are instructed of the Lord that you are to be disfellowshipped and not excommunicated."

She bowed her head and cried and cried and cried. "Yes. I know. I know that this is right. I'm so thankful for a loving God, and a Savior, and for the fact that you brethren have received revelation here today."

We all had a prayer of thanksgiving together, gave her instructions, and ended the disciplinary council.

I had to report to the stake president next. I thought there might be trouble. I told him about everything that had happened and that my counselors and I were completely united in the outcome. The stake president was supportive. "Alright. I find it highly unusual but you're the bishop and I support your decision."

Thereafter, I met with that sister on a regular basis. There were a few slips and bumps, as well as a few things she needed extra help with, but within several months, her life was completely turned around. She continued to be active and faithful in the church. In less than a year she was able to attend the temple with her children.

Discussion Questions

1. How do you feel about this sister's determination to be forgiven and return to the temple?
2. What do you think of the Brigham Young quote in this chapter and how might it apply to you?
3. How do you feel about what happened in the disciplinary council?

CHAPTER 19
More Than Fish

"Simon, son of Jonas, lovest thou me more than these?" (John 21:15)

While I was a bishop in Missouri, a young couple in our ward needed help. They were struggling in several areas of their lives. The husband had a part-time job as a truck driver. They had no children and the wife sometimes traveled with him. The ward helped them get by a few times with funds from fast offerings. We also tried to help them spiritually, and I had a few counseling sessions with them. As they became more active in the church, their overall situation seemed to be improving.

One Sunday, that young husband asked to speak with me privately. We went into my office and sat down. I asked how I could help him. He said that he wanted to thank me for all we had done for him and his wife. He also said that he believed in the church and had very good feelings about it. He wanted to tell me that we would not be seeing them in church much more because he was going to become a professional bass fisherman. Most bass fishing tournaments were held on Sunday, so they would not be very active in the church in the future.

He asked if I understood. I told him that being a professional bass fisherman was a lot like being a professional in any other sport. Very few people who have a desire to make a living in professional sports are able to be successful at it. I asked about his bass fishing background, if he had all the equipment he would need, and if he had a sponsor. He admitted that he had limited amateur experience, little equipment, and no sponsors. I suggested that he might want to consider this decision a little more carefully. He said that his mind was made up and that he was going to take the plunge. Then he asked me if this change would be OK with the Lord and the church.

Rather than giving him my opinion, I offered to read what the Lord had to say about it.

He was very surprised. "You mean the Lord has actually said something about this?"

"Indeed he has." I commenced reading about one of Christ's appearances after his resurrection.

> After these things Jesus shewed himself again to the disciples at the sea of Tiberias; and on this wise shewed he himself. There were together Simon Peter, and Thomas called Didymus, and Nathanael of Cana in Galilee, and the sons of Zebedee, and two other of his disciples. Simon Peter saith unto them, I go a fishing. (John 21:1-3)

Before his call to follow Jesus, Peter had been a professional fisherman. When Peter said, "I go a fishing," he was not talking about sport fishing: he was talking about returning to his former life of professional fishing. It appears that at that point, seven additional disciples were interested in joining him in the fishing business. They said to Peter,

> We also go with thee. They went forth, and entered into a ship immediately; and that night they caught nothing. But when the morning was now come, Jesus stood on the shore: but the disciples knew not that it was Jesus. Then Jesus saith unto them, Children, have ye any meat? They answered him, No. And he said unto them, Cast the net on the right side of the ship, and ye shall find. They cast

therefore, and now they were not able to draw it for the multitude of fishes. Therefore that disciple whom Jesus loved saith unto Peter, It is the Lord. Now when Simon Peter heard that it was the Lord, he … cast himself into the sea. And the other disciples came in a little ship; (for they were not far from land, but as it were two hundred cubits,) dragging the net with fishes. As soon then as they were come to land, they saw a fire of coals there, and fish laid thereon, and bread. Jesus saith unto them, Bring of the fish which ye have now caught. Simon Peter went up, and drew the net to land full of great fishes … Jesus saith unto them, Come and dine … Jesus then cometh, and taketh bread, and giveth them, and fish likewise. (John 21:3-13)

Isn't it interesting that the resurrected Jesus built a fire on the beach, cooked a breakfast of fish and bread, and served it to his disciples? We could learn much from His example: the Savior did not consider himself too great to build fires, cook, and serve.

Returning to John's account, it says, "This is now the third time that Jesus shewed himself to his disciples, after that he was risen from the dead. So when they had dined, Jesus saith to Simon Peter, Simon, son of Jonas, lovest thou me more than these?" (John 21:15)

Jesus asked Peter if he loved him more than what? More than fish. More than fishing. More than the fishing business. Peter responded,

Yea, Lord; thou knowest that I love thee. He saith unto him, Feed my lambs. He saith to him again the second time, Simon, son of Jonas, lovest thou me? He saith unto him, Yea, Lord; thou knowest that I love thee. He saith unto him, Feed my sheep. He saith unto him the third time, Simon, son of Jonas, lovest thou me? Peter was grieved because he said unto him the third time, Lovest thou me? And he said unto him, Lord, thou knowest all things; thou knowest that I love thee. Jesus saith unto him, Feed my sheep. (John 21:15-17)

Take note that Jesus gave Peter three opportunities to affirm his love. This appears to be a tender mercy giving Peter an opportunity to supersede his previous three denials.

After reading and explaining John's account to the young man in my office I said, "You now know what the Lord said about a circumstance similar to yours. Let me ask you a question, 'Do you love the Lord more than fish?'" He replied that he was shocked to know that the Lord had ever said anything about that topic and said that he would need to think about it. That young couple continued to attend church for about another month and then moved from the area. I have been curious since then about what this young man's final answer was to the Lord's question, and about how that answer has impacted the life of his family.

Study Question

1. I firmly believe that each of us needs to ask ourselves the same question, substituting our favorite things in place of the word, fish. "Do I love the Lord more than _____?"

CHAPTER 20
Mothers Die

"And if they die they shall die unto me, and if they live they shall live unto me." (D&C 42:44)

When I was teaching institute in Missouri, a man in his late twenties came to an afternoon class. He asked unusual questions and made some rather bizarre comments. Most of what he said was very negative. After the second time he came, I invited him into my office after class. I asked him how he felt about the church, and he said that he had a lot of bad feelings about it. I suggested that institute class was not the best place to deal with those issues and recommended that instead he have a talk with his bishop. He didn't want to talk to his bishop, but he wanted to tell me why he had negative feelings.

He told me that when he was on his mission, his mother became quite ill. He prayed very sincerely that she would be healed. He promised that he would be the best missionary and person that he could if she was healed.

A few months went by and his mother got worse and died. He was devastated. He asked his mission president to let him go home for the funeral. After some counseling, pondering, and prayer, the mission president said that he felt inspired that his mother and the Lord wanted him to remain in the mission field.

The young man became very angry and told his mission president to jump in the lake. He left his mission and never returned. He was extremely upset with the Lord for allowing his mother to die. He was upset with the mission president for not wanting him to go home. His anger and bitterness grew. He quit attending church and intentionally became in involved in all kinds of sin. I suggested that it was best not to talk to me about those things and that he really needed to be talking with his bishop. He repeated that he did not want to talk to his bishop. Overall, he was very emotional, very negative, and very troubled.

Then he asked me what I thought about all he had told me. I looked across the desk at him. "I think that's the stupidest thing I've ever heard."

"What?"

I repeated, "I think that's the stupidest thing I've ever heard."

He jumped up, red faced. I thought he was going to climb across the desk and clobber me. He screamed, "How dare you say that to me?"

I leaned forward and said, very firmly, "Everyone's mother dies! My mother died. Your mother died. If none of us can keep our testimonies when our mothers die, then no one can believe in God, or stay in the church. What you just told me is the stupidest thing I've ever heard because you have failed to accept the basic fact that everyone's mother dies, sooner or later, no matter what."

He sat down. He was quiet for a while. Finally he said, "Well, maybe I better go talk to my bishop." A short time later, his bishop told me that he was meeting with him and some progress was being made.

Sooner or later we will all have loved ones die. We need to be spiritually prepared to deal with it in such a way that we will be worthy to live with them in the next life.

Prophetic Insight

Joseph Smith taught: "The spirits of the just are exalted to a greater and more glorious work; hence they are blessed in their departure to the world of spirits. Enveloped in flaming fire, they are not far from us, and know and understand our thoughts, feelings, and motions, and are often pained therewith." *History of the Church*, 5:390; *The Best of Joseph and Brigham*, GVS, 99)

Discussion Questions

1. When someone you love dies, how do you plan to deal with it?
2. What do you need to do to be worthy to live with your loved ones when you get to the other side of the veil?

CHAPTER 21
Pride and Humility

"O that cunning plan of the evil one! O the vainness, and the frailties, and the foolishness of men! When they are learned they think they are wise, and they hearken not unto the counsel of God, for they set it aside, supposing they know of themselves... But to be learned is good if they hearken unto the counsels of God." (2 Nephi 9:28-29)

Pride

Ron was friendly until I was called to be bishop. Then I noticed that our relationship became somewhat strained. I gradually realized that Ron had a problem dealing with anyone in authority. Since I had become an authority figure, his attitude toward me had changed. But in many ways he was a good man. He was very intelligent, well-educated, and enjoyed serving others.

One day, he and I were called on to give a blessing together to an older brother in our ward. Both of us had some negative feelings about this man because he had been abusive to his wife. The brother had fallen on ice and sustained a serious head injury.

After we arrived at the home, Ron did the anointing and I sealed the anointing. In the sealing part of the blessing, I was surprised to feel inspired to bless the man that he was going to have a full recovery. He was quite old, his injury was serious, and I knew him to be an abusive husband. I thought his wife might be better off without him, but as I gave the blessing I felt a definite inspiration to bless him that he would be healed.

Then something happened that I had never experienced before. My hands were on his head and Ron's hands were on top of mine. In the middle of the blessing, Ron raised his hands up off of my hands. Of course I noticed that he had raised his hands and I hesitated briefly. Then, not knowing what else to do, I just went ahead and finished the blessing.

Later, I mentioned to Ron that I didn't understand what happened. He did not want to talk about it. I was left with the impression that he didn't agree with what I was saying so he raised his hands in protest, declining to continue to participate in the blessing. Subsequently, the elderly brother made a surprisingly quick recovery and regained his full health.

Another experience with Ron came soon afterward. Ron served as Sunday School teacher for the 16-18 year old youth in our ward. In his teaching he used a very intellectual approach. He usually employed a "devil's advocate" teaching method, inserting comments that did not necessarily agree either with his own real opinion or with church doctrine. Several different parents of the youth in his class came to me and expressed their concern that Ron's teaching was destroying faith rather than building it. They were uncomfortable with him as a teacher. After several people talked to me, and after I did some investigation, I knew I had to do something to correct the situation.

I asked Ron to meet with me privately in the bishop's office. I told him that some of the youth in his class and some of their parents were concerned about his methods of teaching, as well as some of the things he taught. He responded that he felt good about what he was teaching and the way he was teaching it. He also stated emphatically that he was going to continue teaching just the same as he had been.

Sadly, I had to be more direct. "You know, Ron, you're entitled to believe what you want and in some situations teach what you want, but not on the Lord's time, and not in the Lord's house, and not in the Lord's Sunday School. All of us need to teach things that go along with the manual. If you are going to continue teaching, you need to do so in a way that is appropriate and faith-building."

He became quite agitated. "You know, you're only telling me this because we used to be friends. You're taking advantage of that and letting your own opinions interfere."

"Ron, it does not matter who is sitting in this bishop's chair. Whether it's me or somebody else, if a teacher in a class is teaching something that is detrimental to the students and not in line with the established curriculum, then that has to be corrected. It has nothing to do with personalities or whatever our history is or isn't, this is just the way it needs to be."

He was unmoved. "Well, I'm just going to do it the way I want to do it."

I was very concerned. "I'm sorry, but you don't have that option. You can do it the Lord's way or you cannot do it."

Ron raised his voice. "You wouldn't dare release me over something like this!"

"I'm sorry, but if you insist on going ahead in a way that's inappropriate, then you don't leave me any other option."

Then the Spirit prompted me to say something more. "Ron, in addition to the Sunday School class, I'm concerned that you may be using these same teaching methods to teach your own family. I know that you and your wife are very strong in the faith, but you have two teenage children. If you teach them the way you have been teaching Sunday School, it may weaken their testimonies and cause them to become inactive in the church."

He angrily responded that the way he taught his Sunday School class, and especially his own children, was none of my business. Then he stood up, swore at me, opened the door so hard that it slammed a hole in the wall, and stomped out.

Ron had to be released as the teacher and we called somebody else. Subsequently, I tried to approach Ron on several occasions, but was rebuffed. Over time his family's church attendance became less regular. I am sad to report that within two years, both of Ron's children became inactive in the church. Many times I hoped and prayed that things would eventually get better for Ron and his family.

Humility

A few months after Ron's angry exit from my office, a woman in our ward, Pat, came to speak with me. She began, "Bishop, I need to talk to you about something that's very important." She told me that Ron was her home teacher, which I already knew. He had done many things for her and her son as their home teacher, which she very much appreciated. Pat was a good woman, but she struggled with several personal issues. She had no husband, and her life centered around her teenage son, Jeb.

Pat cried as she explained, "I love Ron but when he gives us home teaching lessons, it is destructive to our faith. I think I can handle it, but I'm worried about my son. I don't want him exposed to such teaching. Will you please remove Ron as my home teacher, but don't tell him why?"

I was sad about that, but I asked the high priest group leader to make the change and it was done.

A few months later, the sister who had been our ward organist moved away. We were a small ward and had no one to replace her. Jeb was an excellent piano player, even though he was only 15 years old. After significant prayer, I felt inspired to call Jeb into my office and ask him if he would be willing to serve as our ward organist.

He looked surprised. "Bishop, I don't play the organ."

"I know that, Jeb. But, I think you can learn and I've arranged for someone in another ward to give you organ lessons. They are willing to do it for free. I would like you to begin playing in sacrament meeting next week. Play the organ just as if it were a piano. Don't use the pedals. Start taking the organ lessons and work in organ skills as soon as you are able. Are you willing?"

"Yes, bishop. This is daunting to me, but I am willing to do it."

I assured him that the Lord would help him. It was only a few months until he was playing the organ well.

A few years later, Jeb was one of my institute students. He went on a mission, was married in the temple, and now has a happy family. Pat eventually overcame many of her problems, remained dedicated to the church, and enjoyed more happiness in her life. She especially loves to visit her faithful son Jeb and his family.

Pat was a humble and courageous mother. She was raising a humble and courageous son. She was motivated by her love of the gospel and her family. Those who let pride cloud their vision and teaching could learn much from her.

Ron was a great man in many ways. But his unwillingness to accept correction from those called to serve as leaders in the Church became a stumbling block to him and had a negative effect on his family.

Each of us, over time, will probably have a church leader we don't really like. It will be up to us to decide if we will let our personal dislike of that leader become a barrier to our progression. Pride will prevent us from receiving the blessings promised to the humble and obedient.

Discussion Questions

1. Why is it usually beneficial to have a good attitude toward authority figures?
2. Why is it imperative to teach in a way that builds faith?
3. In what ways did Ron exhibit pride?
4. How did Pat and Jeb manifest faith and humility?
5. How will pride and humility affect your life?

CHAPTER 22
Broken Cisterns

"They have forsaken me the fountain of living waters, and hewed them out cisterns, broken cisterns, that hold no water." (Jeremiah 2:13)

During the time I served as a bishop, I also served as the Church Educational System (CES) Coordinator in that area. Therefore, I was in the unique position of being the bishop, institute director, and seminary supervisor, all at the same time. Sometimes I dealt with problems within my ward from the different perspectives of those several responsibilities. This account deals with just such a situation.

A couple in our ward came to talk with me about their daughter, a sophomore in high school. She was a very good player on the high school girls' basketball team. The coach was changing from having one-a-day to two-a-day practices: one in the morning before school and another after school. Because of this change in her practice schedule, she was not going to be able to attend early morning seminary. I immediately had a bad feeling about that. I asked about possible options. There just was not another good option for seminary attendance. The basketball coach had said that anyone who did not attend both practices would be spending most of her time on the bench. I felt inspired to tell the parents that I thought it was very important for her to stay in early morning seminary.

They were deeply concerned. "Bishop, you don't understand. She is a good enough player that we expect she will get a basketball scholarship to attend college. We can't really afford to pay tuition for college and so the only way she can go is on a basketball scholarship. She has to miss seminary in order to play basketball so that she will be able to attend college."

At that instant, I distinctly felt a prompting from the Lord to say, "No, you don't understand. If she doesn't continue to attend seminary, she won't be going to college."

They were taken aback. "This is a family decision and we just came to tell you what we are going to do. We did not come for you to tell us what we should do."

"I understand that it is your choice, but as your bishop, I've told you what I feel inspired to say."

They left my office and no more was said about it. She started going to morning basketball practice and quit attending seminary. In less than a year she was pregnant, had a difficult time finishing high school, had serious problems with her boyfriend, and became completely inactive in the Church. She did not play basketball her remaining high school years, and did not attend college. Basketball was gone. College was gone. Her activity in the church was gone. Many hopes and dreams had disappeared.

Here is a somewhat similar and equally sad story. A really good family in our ward had a son who was a senior in high school. He was a good young man and had been very active in our youth activities. Then he got a job at a local supermarket and started missing youth activities because of his work schedule. I became concerned with his excessive absences from activities. I talked with him and encouraged him to attend when he could, but most of the time he missed. However, things still seemed to be going pretty well for him.

Then one day, his parents showed up in the bishop's office, "We just wanted you to know that the market where our son works has asked him to work on Sundays. If he does not, his hours will be cut way back. We've decided to go ahead and allow him to work on Sundays. We just want you to know that it's not because he's going inactive or has a problem. He just needs to work on Sunday."

I felt prompted to say, "I don't feel good about him working on Sundays. I think it would be better for him to take the cut in hours."

"No, you don't understand. All the money from this job is going to be saved for his mission and there is no other way we can afford to pay for his mission."

Once again, I felt a strong prompting to say, "No you don't understand. If he works on Sunday and misses coming to Church, he won't be going on a mission."

Their mouths dropped open. "What do you mean?"

"I feel inspired to tell you that he shouldn't do this and that if he does, he probably won't be going on a mission."

The parents insisted, "But there's no other way to pay for it. We just don't have the money."

"If you don't have the money for his mission, the ward will help. We will supplement whatever funds you do have so that there will be sufficient for his mission."

"We don't feel very good about that. We think that it is his job, and our job to provide the money."

I wanted them to feel my support, but also to understand the significance that church attendance would have on their son's mission preparation. "I understand, and that is a noble way to feel. But in this case, the ward would like to help pay for his mission in order for him to continue to come to Church."

After a few moments of silence, they said, "We didn't come to ask for your counsel about this. We just came to tell you that this is what we're going to do and why."

The young man started working on Sundays. The ward continued trying to help him and his parents, but sadly, he became totally inactive in the church and never did go on a mission. The rest of his family remained active.

Despite these two sad stories and others that I have not mentioned, many wonderful things also happened while I was a bishop. There were great successes when people had faith and followed counsel. While pondering the many different situations I dealt with as a bishop, I have often thought that when a bishop feels inspired to tell members of his ward something, it would be wise for them to pay close attention. I understand that this isn't always easy. When a bishop or anyone else tells you that you're wrong, it is human nature to feel defensive and angry. But if you can allow the possibility that you could be wrong and your bishop could be right, you will gain access to a very good source of inspired guidance. When you are given counsel, you should seriously consider and pray about that counsel and get your own spiritual confirmation from the Lord. My experience has been that it is usually not a good plan to go against the advice of a bishop. I know that bishops aren't perfect. I wasn't perfect. I know that bishops can make mistakes. I made mistakes. However, I know that most of the time bishops give inspired counsel that will bless the lives of those who are willing to cast aside doubt or pride to follow that counsel.

Discussion Questions:

1. Why is it usually a good idea to seek wise and inspired counsel concerning important decisions?

2. What would you do differently if you were in a situation similar to the two given above?

3. How do the words of Jeremiah relate to these examples and this discussion? "They have forsaken me the fountain of living waters, and hewed them out cisterns, broken cisterns, that hold no water." (Jeremiah 2:13)

CHAPTER 23
Joyful Endurance

"And they shall pass by the angels, and the gods, which are set there, to their exaltation and glory in all things, as hath been sealed upon their heads, which glory shall be a fulness and a continuation of the seeds forever and ever." (D&C 132:19)

While serving as a bishop, I had a wonderful association with an older couple in our ward, Wilbur and Mary Murray. I saw them as pioneers for that area as far as the Church presence was concerned. They were living there before any stakes were formed. They had worked with the mission and served in small branches. In addition, they fulfilled many important church responsibilities and accomplished many wonderful things to help move forward the work of the Lord and His Church in the southwest Missouri area.

They were both sweet and wonderful people. It was always a pleasure to interact with them because of their love for the Lord and for all the people in that area. Every time I saw them, they seemed to glow. They had some health problems incident to age. One day, Wilbur was admitted to the hospital with a serious illness. The doctors said that the situation was grave and that he might not survive. The illness was causing him a considerable amount of pain and suffering.

One night, at about 10:00 p.m., I had a feeling that I should go to the hospital and visit Wilbur. I got up, dressed in some nice clothes, and went to the hospital. I had visited him previously, so I already knew what room he was in. Visiting hours were over, so I just acted like I was supposed to be there and went straight to his room. This particular area had an abundance of ministers who regularly made hospital visits, so that may have been why nobody challenged me. When I entered Wilbur's room, I could see that he was sobbing. I quietly walked over and silently stood by his bed. I reached out and held his hand as he continued to sob.

After a few minutes, I sat down at his bedside. Eventually his crying diminished. I expressed how saddened I was by the great difficulty and pain he was going through. I felt that the Spirit had prompted me to be there that night to help comfort him.

As I attempted to soothe him, he interrupted me. "No, Bishop. You don't understand. I wasn't crying tears of sorrow or suffering. The Lord has blessed me with so much in my life. I have had so many blessings and wonderful things in my life. I was just laying here thinking about all these things and praying to the Lord, thanking him for all that he has blessed me with. I was overcome with joy. When you came in, I was not crying tears of sorrow or pain, but of happiness. Yes, it's true that I'm in a lot of pain and I'm probably near death, but that's not what I'm thinking about. I'm thinking about how blessed I've been." Then suddenly the Spirit washed over me in what felt like great waves and I realized that I wasn't there to comfort him. The Spirit had called me there for Wilbur Murray to comfort me.

We spent a few more minutes crying and praying together. Soon he became sleepy, and so I left that sacred space and went home. But I left a different and better person than when

I arrived. I will never forget the lesson that Wilbur taught me that night.

Wilbur unexpectedly recovered and came home from the hospital. He regained much of his health and he and his wife were well enough to come to church. They served as greeters in our ward, and what wonderful greeters they were! I believe everyone felt a little more loved after being greeted at church by Wilbur and Mary.

A few months later, Mary was not feeling well. They asked if I would come to their home to give her a blessing. It was pleasant to go and visit with them because of their great appreciation and love for each other. Even though they were loved by many, they had never been able to have children. Therefore, there was no immediate family to take care of them in their old age. As I laid my hands on Mary's head to give her a blessing I had an unusual impression that I had never had before and have not had since. It said, "No, you need to bless both of them together."

I stopped and took my hands off her head. "I'm sorry, but I feel that I need to give you both a blessing at the same time. Will you please come sit together?" They did, and I laid one hand on each head and proceeded to give the blessing as I had felt inspired to do.

At first, it was a blessing of healing and comfort. Then the Spirit told me very clearly the blessings that I was supposed to pronounce. I told them that the covenants and promises they had made and received in the temple were still in force and would be fulfilled. I was inspired to remind them that one of the ordinances they had received was the covenant of eternal marriage, which includes the blessing of an eternal posterity. I blessed them that even though they had not had seed or posterity in mortality, that they would indeed have an eternal posterity that would be infinite in number. I blessed them that they would have all the blessings of being a mother and a father and that the time would come when the time spent in mortality would seem very short. The blessing included many other profound things and by the time it was done, all three of us were weeping tears of joy.

I have always been grateful to have had the opportunity to be friends with and serve with such wonderful people. About a year later Mary, passed away as she was conversing with beings from beyond the veil who came to get her. Not long after that I moved to another area and lost track of Wilbur, but I know that he remained faithful and "endured to the end." I also know that the Lord rewards good and faithful servants, and that temple covenants are honored in the next life.

Before Mary passed on, Wilbur came to my office and said he needed to talk with me. He explained that he had had a very vivid dream that he wanted me to help him understand. He dreamed that he was in the spirit world. In the dream, he was taken to a large hole that was about 200 yards long and about 100 yards wide. The hole was quite deep and was completely filled with thousands of people standing close together. He had the understanding that he was supposed to help them out of the hole. He felt like it was much more than he could do and that he needed help. He decided that he would ask me to help him. And then he woke up.

As soon as he told me the dream, the meaning was given to me by the Spirit. I told him that it would not be long before he would pass through the veil. One of the main things he would have to do in the spirit world would be missionary work. He cried joyfully. "Oh, I love missionary work."

I explained to him that those in the hole represented people with whom he would share the gospel, and that his help was greatly needed there. He was thrilled.

Then I said, "There is one more very important thing. When you are there and you feel like you need help, do not come back here to get me." We looked in each others' eyes and laughed.

Then he looked at me seriously. "OK bishop, I won't," and then we hugged.

Discussion Questions

1. When have you been comforted by someone in a way that you were not expecting?
2. What are you willing to do in order to experience the kind of joy that Wilbur explained?
3. In what ways would you like to be like Wilbur and Mary Murray?
4. How do you exercise faith in the promise of eternal family relationships?
5. How do you feel about missionary work in the spirit world?

CHAPTER 24
Prayer for Speed

"And now, my son, I trust that I shall have great joy in you, because of your steadiness and your faithfulness unto God; for as you have commenced in your youth to look to the Lord your God, even so I hope that you will continue in keeping his commandments; for blessed is he that endureth to the end." (Alma 38:2)

Ross was a former student of mine. He and his wife had become close friends of our family. Sadly, he and his wife were having marital trouble. They had been married about a year and seemed to have a deep commitment to each other. However, they fought over many things. Several times, they came to our home to counsel with my wife and me. Sometimes I would go to one room with Ross, while Barbra would go to another room with his wife: they were too volatile when they were together.

One time I was downstairs with Ross. Barbra was upstairs on the other end of the house with his wife. My seventeen-year-old son, Mike, was upstairs in his bedroom, politely trying to stay out of their business. As I talked with Ross, he became more and more agitated. I tried to calm him down, but it just wasn't working. Things suddenly took a turn for the worse. He jumped up and wildly ran up the stairs, through the house, and out the front door. Fearing that he was in a frame of mind such that he could be a danger to himself, I ran after him. He crashed out the front door with me close behind, imploring him to stop. He ran across the front lawn and down the street, screaming and crying as he went. I felt like I needed to catch him and help him calm down. As I ran after him, I felt love for him as if he were my own son.

I was barefoot. As I ran down the street as fast and hard as I could, my feet really started to hurt. Even though I was running as fast as I could, Ross was faster. By the time we were down the street about seventy-five yards, I could see that he was pulling away. I was getting tired and my feet hurt more and more with every step. So I prayed one of the most anxious, desperate prayers of my life. I prayed that the Lord would give me strength and speed to catch Ross and help him to be safe. I felt a surge of hope and faith and was able to exert an even greater effort as my speed increased. But a few steps later, it became obvious that my prayer wasn't being answered in the way that I had expected. I was slowing again, and the distance between Ross and me was rapidly increasing. I was almost overwhelmed with surprise, disappointment, and misery. Tears began to flow. I knew that I had failed to rescue Ross. For some reason, my prayers had not been answered.

Just then, Mike, who had been in his bedroom upstairs, came out of nowhere and blasted by me in a full sprint. He passed me like I was standing still. He also had bare feet but his speed amazed me. He didn't know what had happened, but heard us go out the front door and had a strong feeling that he needed to help. He didn't say a word or look back, but I knew my prayer for greater strength and speed had been answered. It was not long before he caught Ross and carefully tackled him onto some grass by the side of the road. When I managed to catch up a few minutes later, Ross was lying on the grass, sobbing, with Mike lying across him, attempting to comfort him and holding him there. I lay down with them, hugged Ross, and spoke soothingly to him. He hugged me back. A few minutes later, Mike, Ross, and I walked back to our house with our arms around each others' shoulders.

Ross needed some counseling. The crisis passed, and the marriage not only remained intact, but improved. We felt increased love for him and his wife.

Let me explain more about Mike. He was my youngest son and we shared an unusual bond. We did many things together: shooting, fishing, canoeing, hiking, basketball, and lots more. All of my other children had left the nest, but he remained and was a great joy in my life. However, before the incident with Ross happened, he and I had been having some conflict. Looking back, I can see that some of the troubles were typical things related to growing up. However, part of it was my fault. Because he was my youngest son, I was having a hard time letting go of him as a child and accepting that he was becoming a man.

As Mike shot past me on the road that day, not only was I grateful that he was there to help, but I had a powerful feeling sweep over me. Suddenly I knew in my heart that Mike was no longer to be treated as a child, but as a man. From that day on, the strain in our relationship diminished and the bond between us grew. It continued to be a bond between father and son, but it now includes a bond of friendship that has continued to grow and bless our lives as the years go by.

Discussion Questions

1. If you ever feel like Ross did, what are some better ways to cope with it?

2. What can be learned from this experience about faith, prayers, and about answers that come through others?

3. What can you learn from this experience about parenting and friendship?

CHAPTER 25

Keys to Learning

"Let not all be spokesmen at once; but let one speak at a time and let all listen unto his sayings..." (D&C 88:122)

In my lifetime of teaching, I have observed that some students learn more and are changed more by what they learn than others. Those students have certain good habits in common. Following are five keys to help you be a more effective gospel student.

You Don't Know Everything

One of the most important keys is for students to start out with the understanding that they do not know everything. Some may think that's obvious, but I have noticed that it is not obvious to some children. Often I have observed parents trying to teach something to a child and heard the child say something like, "Oh, I already know that." At times like that I often think, "Duh, if you already knew and applied it then they would not be talking about it."

Understanding and application begins with the admission that you don't know it all and that there are many important things that you need to learn. So whether you are a youth or adult, if somebody starts to teach you something and you are thinking you already know it, there is a good chance that you are wrong. At such times you should try to put aside your pride and adopt the humility to listen and see if there is something for you to learn and apply. Stated simply, the first key to being a good student is to not think that you already know.

Joseph Smith said,

> If we get puffed up by thinking that we have much knowledge, we are apt to get a contentious spirit, and correct knowledge is necessary to cast out that spirit. The evil of being puffed up with correct, though useless, knowledge is not so great as the evil of contention. (*History of the Church*, 5:340)

Notice that Joseph stated that being proudly puffed up with knowledge is evil. Then he goes on to say that contention is worse, which leads me to the next key.

Avoid Contention

Jesus taught,

> And there shall be no disputations among you, as there have hitherto been; neither shall there be disputations among you concerning the points of my doctrine, as there have hitherto been. For verily, verily I say unto you, he that hath the spirit of contention is not of me, but is of the devil, who is the father of contention, and he stirreth up the hearts of men to contend with anger, one with another. Behold, this is not my doctrine, to stir up the hearts of men with anger, one against another; but this is my doctrine, that such things should be done away. (3 Nephi 11:29-30)

Could Jesus have said that any more powerfully? And yet, most of us have sat in church classes where there's been contention. This is His church, and He said, if there's contention, "It is not of me, but it is of the devil." If you want to say something contentious in a class, you need to stop and think about whose side you are on. There is the Lord's side and the devil's.

Contention is on the devil's side. It doesn't matter if you think the other person is wrong. It doesn't even matter if they are definitely wrong. Contention is to be avoided. Contention is a greater evil than saying something wrong. I'm afraid that a lot of people don't understand that, even though Jesus and Joseph Smith taught it very clearly.

Here is an example from a Gospel Doctrine class in Missouri. It was taught by a very good and well-prepared teacher. She taught that it was Jehovah speaking in Moses chapter two. An older brother in the back raised his hand and said that what she was teaching was wrong because God referred to his Only Begotten Son. The teacher responded that she was following the manual. (*Old Testament Gospel Doctrine Teacher's Manual* (2002), 1) The brother argued that it was clearly wrong no matter what the manual said. Another brother spoke up and agreed with the first brother. The teacher turned to me and asked if I could help. I was upset by the two students' behavior. I asked them if they knew about the doctrine of divine investiture of authority. They did not. I told them that it was a well-known doctrine which had been clarified in a 1916 *Doctrinal Exposition by The First Presidency and the Twelve*, which stated that a member of the godhead or even an angel could speak in the first person for another divine entity. The first brother said that he had never heard of such a thing. I referred him to Appendix 2 of the book, *Articles of Faith* by James E. Talmage. I said that the doctrine of divine investiture of authority is obvious because the Holy Ghost often speaks in first person for the Father and the Son. I told him I was surprised that he would be so contentious regarding something he knew so little about. The teacher thanked me and continued the lesson without further interruption. Thereafter, both of those brethren refrained from such outbursts, for which the rest of the class was grateful. I probably should have handled that situation more gently, but at the time I was irritated by their disrespect for teacher and the doctrine. Apparently ours was not the only class that had trouble with this issue because the entire "Doctrinal Exposition" was soon republished in the April 2002 *Ensign*, on pages 12-18.

Another time in Missouri, I had a large institute class with a new student who seemed intent on impressing his girlfriend. He interrupted me to say that what I had just taught was wrong and why. I smiled and said, "Thank you very much for that opinion," and went on with the lesson.

The next day the president of the institute student council came to my office and said that he had looked it up and found that I was right and the other student was wrong. I smiled and said, "Yes, I know that and could easily have corrected him last night."

"Then why didn't you?"

"Usually it is better to avoid contention than to prove you are right. Besides, I didn't want to embarrass him in front of the class and his girlfriend." Thereafter, the president took it upon himself to tell everyone what had happened, what he had learned, and what I had said. Even though I did not know in advance or approve of him passing the story on, it turned out to have a very beneficial effect on the class.

Let One Speak at a Time

The next key I would like to discuss is based on the following scripture: "Appoint among yourselves a teacher, and let not all be spokesmen at once; but let one speak at a time and let all listen unto his sayings, that when all have spoken that all may be edified of all, and that every man may have an equal privilege." (Doctrine and Covenants 88:122)

In church classes, it is appropriate to have discussion and to have different people say different things, but there is one major rule. Only one person speaks at a time. Have you ever sat in a class where more than one person spoke at a time? It's not the Lord's way. It should never happen in a church class, unless you are having some kind of group activity. I've been in youth classes where there was so much talking going on that the teacher could not give the lesson. I've been in adult classes where there was so much talking that it was distracting and difficult to follow the lesson. Listen to the person who is speaking. Comment when appropriate. But let one speak at a time.

Be Reverent

Reverence is prerequisite to good teaching. There must be reverence before spiritual learning can take place. If I am ever called on to teach in the deacons', teachers' or priests' quorum, one of the first things I will say is, "Please quit tipping your chairs against the wall, sit still, and be quiet." And if they are not willing to do that, they might have to have a discussion with their parents or the Bishop. Their parents might have to sit with them in class. There should be no irreverence or disrespect.

When I supervised seminary teachers in Missouri, one early morning seminary teacher was having a lot of trouble with her class. She wasn't a great teacher or a poor teacher, but she was a good teacher. There are big differences between teachers. Some are going to teach in a way or in a style that's very interesting and appealing to you. There are going to be others that you don't find interesting or appealing.

In that seminary class were three basically good young men. They kept the commandments and were active in the church. However, they decided they didn't like their teacher and the way she taught. They started being irreverent and disruptive in her class. They figured that it was their right to misbehave. In their opinion, the teacher wasn't any good and therefore they didn't have to listen. The teacher came to me as her supervisor. "I can't teach my seminary class. I've got three boys in there that just won't let me do it."

I gathered more information, then requested a meeting with the three young men, their parents, and the bishop. In the meeting, I told the young men what the teacher had reported and asked what they had to say for themselves. They said that they did not like her and did not think she was a good teacher. They did not feel bad about their behavior because her lessons were boring. That made some of the parents very uncomfortable.

I asked them individually, "Have you ever prayed for your teacher?" None had. I continued, "Tell me anything you have said or done to help your teacher or to make your class better." They had done nothing. "Okay, here's the deal: you go back to class. You pray for your teacher, and you go in willing to help her. If you do that, you are going to start liking the class and everything is going to be fine. Will you do it?" Two of the boys said they would. One of the boys was unwilling to commit.

The next day they all went back to class. The two boys who committed to pray for and help the teacher lived up to their promise. The other boy continued to disrupt the class. I called his parents to tell them that their son had lost the privilege of attending early morning seminary. They would need to have a home study class with him, to which they agreed. The two boys who prayed for and helped their teacher ended up having a great experience in seminary. So did the teacher and the whole class. The two young men went on to graduate from seminary, go on missions, and be married in the temple.

Some people might think that this situation should have been handled more softly. To them I would say, "This is serious.

Peoples' souls are on the line." Consider the following quote by Joseph Smith:

> No man or woman shall be interrupted who is appointed to speak by any disorderly person or persons in the congregation by whispering, by laughing, by talking, by menacing gestures, by getting up and running out in a disorderly manner or by offering indignity to the worship or the religion, to any teacher or officer of the church, in anywise whatsoever by any display of ill manners or ill breeding from old to young, rich or poor, male or female, bond or free, black or white, believer or unbeliever, and if any of the above insults are offered, such measures will be taken as are lawful, to punish the transgressor or aggressors and eject them from the house." (*History of the Church*; 2:368-369)

Participate Appropriately

As a student, say something, participate, but not too much and not in the wrong way. Other people have good things to say. The teacher has things to say. If you are talking more than anyone else then you need to cut back.

Also, be careful that when you do talk you are not just expressing opinions. It's fine to talk about your experiences or insights, but keep your doctrinal opinions to yourself. It is better to listen to somebody who actually knows the answer than to express an unfounded opinion. Brigham Young said it this way:

> All do not stop and reflect, neither do they fully understand the principles of the gospel, the principles of the Holy Priesthood, and from this cause, many imbibe the idea that they are capable of leading out and teaching principles that have never been taught. They are not aware that the moment they give way to this hallucination, the devil has power over them to lead them on to unholy ground... (*Journal of Discourses*, 3:316-327)

In church classes it is inappropriate to express your opinions as doctrine. That's unholy ground. When you make a statement it should be based on scripture or revelation rather than opinion. Spend valuable class time talking about what we do know, instead of what we don't know.

The quality of a lesson is greatly affected by the quality of the students. One or two outstanding students can make the difference between a poor or great lesson. I once taught an institute class that included an amazing student who seemed to be consistently inspired to say just the right thing to lead into the next point we needed to cover.

I want you to know that I love teaching and I love students. I've had many great teaching experiences. The Lord has given us some rules and some guidelines about learning and teaching. If we follow them, we can have wonderful, spiritually uplifting classes.

Study Questions

1. If you are guilty of violating any of the five keys in this chapter, what are you going to do about it?
2. In the future how are you going to help your teacher?
3. How do you feel about avoiding contention and sticking with sound doctrine?

CHAPTER 26
Keys to Effective Teaching

"Wherefore, he that preacheth and he that receiveth, understand one another, and both are edified and rejoice together." (D&C 50:22)

There are many key aspects of good teaching. I would like to list and explain seven which have been especially helpful to me and to the teachers I have supervised.

Teach by the Spirit

The Lord has stated that we will not be able to successfully teach spiritual things if we do not have the Spirit. "And the Spirit shall be given unto you by the prayer of faith; and if ye receive not the Spirit ye shall not teach." (D&C 42:14)

After many years of teaching in church settings, I was asked by a friend if I would substitute for him in a college history class. Even though I was well-prepared, I was shocked by what a weak teacher I was in a non-Spirit setting. There is a vast difference between teaching with the Holy Ghost and teaching without him. You can feel it, and so can the class.

It is essential to seek and follow the Spirit during all phases of lesson preparation and presentation. It is specifically essential in accomplishing the other steps of effective teaching given below.

Decide What to Teach

Carefully deciding what to teach may be the most important part of teaching. Many teachers spend most of their time teaching the wrong things. Sometimes this is because they spend too much time on minor things and simply run out of time to address the major things. More often the problem is that they have not carefully considered what is most important to teach in that particular lesson. For example, many lessons start out with a readiness question or attention activity. If you spend a third of the lesson time on the readiness part before you even get to the meat of the lesson then you are spending too much time teaching the wrong thing. If the lesson is about certain chapters in Isaiah and you spend half the time talking about the historical context of Isaiah, the definition of symbolism, fashion issues or other details, then you are spending too much time talking about the less important things.

Don't try to teach every single point covered in the lesson manual. Carefully identify the doctrines and principles in the lesson material that will be most beneficial to your students, and spend most of your time teaching those things. Ask yourself, "What do I love about this lesson?" As you are thinking about these two issues, read the scriptural or prophetic statements that the lesson is based on and study related scriptures and references. Then study the lesson manual. Mark or make an outline of the major lesson points and references in the order you intend to use them.

Decide How You are Going to Teach

The lesson manual often makes helpful suggestions on how to teach a particular doctrine, but there may be better ways to teach the lesson than those listed. There are many different teaching methods. See *Teaching, No Greater Call,* and *Come, Follow Me: Learning Resources for Youth* for ideas. You should be willing and able to teach using a variety of methods. Prayerfully consider which methods will work best with the specific lesson and class. Sometimes a teaching style that works great in one class will flop in another. Involving students in class discussion is usually preferable to lecture, but not always.

Avoid methods that detract from the main principles of the lesson or that are inappropriate and would offend the Spirit. Sharing personal experiences can be effective, but be very careful about sharing anything too personal or embarrassing about yourself or others. Some students will use your past sins to excuse their own. Therefore, even though you have repented for past serious transgressions, you should steer clear of discussing them, especially with younger students.

If you are not well prepared or if you are giving a lesson or talk on short notice, do not mention your lack of preparation. Never say you are not prepared or blame anyone else, especially the bishopric. Also, never suggest that you would rather not be teaching or speaking. If you are excited about teaching and about the lesson, your students will be more excited to learn.

Remember the Power of the Word

And now, as the preaching of the word had a great tendency to lead the people to do that which was just—yea, it had had more powerful effect upon the minds of the people than the sword, or anything else, which had happened unto them—therefore Alma thought it was expedient that they should try the virtue of the word of God. (Alma 31:5)

Because the word of God is so powerful, actually read from the scriptures during lessons, don't just paraphrase. Of course you can paraphrase portions of text that are less relevant to the doctrine you wish to teach in order to move the lesson along, but if you only paraphrase without ever reading directly from the scriptures, much of the power will be lost.

It is fine for you to read the scriptural references if you are an excellent reader. It is also fine to have students read them. However, avoid having anyone read who is not a proficient reader because reading issues could be embarrassing to some class members and have a negative effect on the lesson.

Ask Questions Correctly

Think very carefully about every question you are going to ask, even if it is one from the manual. Write down every question. Then ask yourself, "Why am I asking this question?" Next ask yourself, "What response do I hope to get?" If you don't have a good reason for the question or if it might result in superfluous responses, don't ask it. When you are happy with the question and the probable response, think about every possible response to the question and try to prepare a way to respond to each one. In class, acknowledge every answer and try to give a positive response even if the answer is wrong or not what you expected.

There are some parts of a lesson that a good teacher can wing, meaning get by without specific preparation. But good questions hardly ever happen that way. I attended a class where the teacher was likeable, prepared, knowledgeable, and never taught false doctrine. He typically asked over 30 questions per class and, sadly, he almost never asked a good question. There was never a good class discussion. Even if a student managed to give a good answer to a poor question the teacher usually just moved on to another unfortunate question. An example of an ineffective question is, "How many of us have done the same thing?" This is either a rhetorical question or asks for a specific number, which is a pointless response. Another example of an ineffective question is, "How sorry do you think he was after he did that?" The obvious answer is "very sorry," which does not promote class discussion or personal reflection.

Perhaps you have been in a class where a barrage of ineffective questions such as these has been asked and you have felt the frustration that comes from sitting through such a presentation. Perhaps you have also been in a class where the teacher used a few well-chosen questions that propelled the class into an edifying, Spirit-filled discussion. Choose to be the kind of teacher who prepares effective questions ahead of time. I hope every time you prepare a lesson that in the back of your mind you will remember this axiom, "Never wing a question."

A few good questions (possibly two or three) will usually be enough to sustain an interesting discussion for an entire class period. Here are some examples of good questions: "What insight or experience do you have related to this scripture?" "What principle does this teach you?" "How will you apply this to your life?" "What part of this reference do you know to be true, and how?" "What do you love about this reference, and why?"

One of the most important things about asking questions is that you have to learn to wait for answers. Many good questions require some thought. Often the fastest answers are the worst ones. Most teachers do not wait long enough. Sometimes it is a good idea to say something like, "I am going to give you a few moments to think about this question before I call on anyone." At times you will have to wait so long for class members to respond to a question that it starts to be uncomfortable. But often the students who are slowest to respond give the best answers. Learn to love the quiet time when the Spirit is working to bring forth wonderful responses.

If you have asked a good question resulting in good class discussion, do not stifle it. Sometimes a class following the Spirit will take you in a different direction than expected. Meeting the students' needs and following the Spirit is more important than covering all the material you had planned.

A few last pointers on asking questions. Don't ask a question that can be answered with yes or no. Don't ask questions that are too easy or have obvious answers (this is awkward for everyone). Don't ask questions that are too difficult or controversial. Don't ask factual questions that just require the repeating of facts. Factual questions do not teach those who know the answers and give minimal benefit for those who don't. Don't ask questions that tend to solicit speculative doctrinal opinions. Your purpose is not to teach or solicit opinion—it is to teach correct doctrine. Excellent questions will help focus your lessons on true doctrine and encourage class members to apply that doctrine to their own lives.

Make Sure Everyone Has a Chance to Participate

In order to have good class discussions, it is critical not to have the same few people always answer the questions. Many years ago I was a student in a large Sunday School Gospel Doctrine class. There were two older men in the class who answered nearly every question and made nearly every comment. They talked more than the teacher and totally dominated the class. They were quite argumentative and seemed to be the proud "know it all" type but seldom said anything enlightening. Eventually I was asked to be the teacher of that class. At the beginning of the first class I taught, I announced that I wanted to give more class members an opportunity to participate. I stated that in order to do that, I would accept only two brief responses from any one class member per class. In the first few minutes the same two men spoken up two times each. Thereafter, I did not call on them or accept comments from them. They constantly waved their hands and interrupted during the rest of the class. Each time I smiled and kindly reminded them that they had each already had their two turns and that we wanted to give others a chance to participate. Other than their antics, the class went quite well.

After the class they both confronted me, angry. "We are going to talk. We've got important things to say and these people need to hear it."

"Yes, you can talk and you've got your two turns just like everybody else."

"If that is the way it's going to be then we will quit coming to class."

I told them that I hoped they would keep coming to class. I also told them that they would continue to receive two brief turns just like everyone else.

Before church was over that day, more than thirty people came up to me and expressed their gratitude for what I had done. Beginning the next week, the class started having good discussions and there was a big jump in attendance. The two problem brethren continued to come to class and learned to behave appropriately. This was an extreme case and most of the time such issues can be handled more gently. However, it is critical that class participation involve as many students as possible.

Love Your Students

Near the beginning of one fall semester many years ago, I was irritated at some of the students. I was one of 30 teachers at an institute of religion which was attended by over 6000 students. As I walked around the halls of the institute, I observed several things that were inappropriate. Among other things, some students were dressed immodestly, some seemed to be worldly and some seemed to be very self-centered.

One day while I was feeling disgusted at some students, the Holy Ghost spoke these distinct words in my mind, "They are just trying to make it." At the same time, I felt an increased comprehension that many of these students were struggling with difficult social, academic, financial and spiritual issues. Within a few moments, all my thoughts and feelings of judgment were replaced with love and a greater desire to help. Ever since that time when I begin to be judgmental, I repeat to myself, "They are just trying to make it," and that feeling of love is renewed.

Study Questions

1. What are you willing to do in order to "teach by the Spirit?"
2. Why do you think so many teachers skip deciding what to teach, and why are you going to make sure that you don't?
3. Can you give some examples of correctly composed questions?
4. As a teacher, how can you be more of a light, and less of a judge?

CHAPTER 27
The Divine Principle of Adaptation

"This is the principle on which the government of heaven is conducted—by revelation adapted to the circumstances in which the children of the kingdom are placed." Joseph Smith, (History of the Church, 5:134-135; GVS, The Best of Joseph and Brigham, page 16, quote 21)

When the resurrected Christ appeared to the Nephites, they heard the voice of the Father saying, "Behold my Beloved Son, in whom I am well pleased, in whom I have glorified my name— hear ye him." (3 Nephi 11:7)

Shortly thereafter, Jesus said,

> Behold, I am Jesus Christ whom the prophets testified shall come into the world. And behold, I am the light and life of the world; and I have drunk out of that bitter cup which the Father hath given me, and have glorified the Father in taking upon me the sins of the world, in the which I have suffered the will of the Father in all things from the beginning. (3 Nephi 11:10-11)

After proving his resurrection, giving his Nephite apostles power to act in His name, and teaching them many wonderful things, Jesus declared,

I perceive that ye are weak, that ye cannot understand all my words which I am commanded of the Father to speak unto you at this time. Therefore, go ye unto your homes, and ponder upon the things which I have said, and ask of the Father, in my name, that ye may understand, and prepare your minds for the morrow, and I come unto you again... And it came to pass that when Jesus had thus spoken, he cast his eyes round about again on the multitude, and beheld they were in tears, and did look steadfastly upon him as if they would ask him to tarry a little longer with them. And he said unto them: Behold, my bowels are filled with compassion towards you. Have ye any that are sick among you? Bring them hither. Have ye any that are lame, or blind, or halt, or maimed, or leprous, or that are withered, or that are deaf, or that are afflicted in any manner? Bring them hither and I will heal them, for I have compassion upon you; my bowels are filled with mercy. For I perceive that ye desire that I should show unto you what I have done unto your brethren at Jerusalem, for I see that your faith is sufficient that I should heal you. (3 Nephi 17:2-8)

Let's carefully list and examine some of the things revealed in these verses.

1. Jesus perceived that the people were weak and not able to comprehend the things which the Father had commanded him to teach.

2. Jesus adapted the Father's directive to the circumstances and told the people to go home, prepare themselves, and return the next day for more instruction.

3. Based on the desires, needs, and faith of the people, Jesus then altered the directive he had just given and proceeded to heal all the sick among them at that time.

How could he not teach what he had been commanded to teach by the Father? It was not because he was disobedient. "I do nothing of myself; but as the Father hath taught me, I speak these things. And he that sent me is with me: the Father hath

not left me alone; for I do always those things that please him."
(John 8:28-29; see also Moses 4:2; 2 Nephi 31:7; Mosiah 15:7;
Luke 2:49; John 4:34; Luke 22:42) Jesus, who was "swallowed
up in the will of the Father" and who "always does those things
that please him," chose not to speak all that the Father had
commanded *at that time.*

Then Jesus revoked his own instruction by inviting the sick
to come forward and be healed. When he gave the instruction
to go home and prepare spiritually to learn more, didn't he
know that they already had faith sufficient to be healed? Then
why tell them to go home and then change his mind? There
can only be one reason: the Father and Son were trying to
teach us something. The following statement by the Prophet
Joseph Smith gives us a key, "This is the principle on which the
government of heaven is conducted—by revelation adapted
to the circumstances in which the children of the kingdom
are placed." (*History of the Church,* 5:134-135; EJST, 575) The
principle of adaptation, as demonstrated by Jesus and defined
by Joseph includes observation, feedback, compassion, mercy,
and adaptation.

There are numerous scriptural and historical examples of
the principle of adaptation, but probably the best example
is the implementation and ultimate fulfillment of the Law
of Moses. (JST Exodus 34:1-2; Hebrews 3:10-11; Hebrews
9:15; Hebrews 12:22-24) In the Law of Moses, the Lord gave
instructions that were specifically tailored to the Israelites' level
of faith and gospel knowledge. Then Christ fulfilled the Law
of Moses and his followers were no longer required to live by
many parts of it. Another biblical example is when the Lord
instructed Peter to begin taking the gospel to Gentiles. (Acts
10:9-48) This was a dramatic change in church policy. Here
are two latter-day scriptures which express the principle of

adaptation: "Behold, I am God and have spoken it; these commandments are of me, and were given unto my servants in their weakness, after the manner of their language, that they might come to understanding." (D&C 1:24) "Wherefore, I the Lord, command and revoke, as it seemeth me good." (D&C 56:4)

Instruction about adapting gospel lessons to meet the needs of the students has been given many times, including the following: "It is more important to help class members understand and apply the scriptures than to cover all the lesson material you have prepared." ("Helps for the Teacher," *New Testament: Gospel Doctrine Teacher's Manual,* (2002), v–ix)

Note the similarity between Jesus' adaptability with the Nephites, and what is currently advocated in church classes. He observed that they were not prepared to hear all of his instructions at that time and adapted his teaching to their needs and circumstances, yet some teachers neglect the principle of adaptation and their students' needs in favor of prescribed methods and materials.

In 3 Nephi 17, the Father and Son are clearly teaching that everybody, regardless of position, needs to be compassionate enough to observe, receive feedback, and make adaptations based on the needs and circumstances of their students. I hope you will apply this principle in your teaching if you are a home or visiting teacher, parent, missionary, member-missionary, speaker, or anyone who teaches in a formal class setting in the church. Please note that care must be taken not to use adaptation as an excuse to depart from correct doctrine or approved curricula.

Through a lifetime of teaching, I gained a strong testimony of the principle of adaptation. I believe that one reason the Spirit was often present in my classes is because I was willing to deviate from my lesson plan, as guided by the Spirit and the needs and circumstances of the students.

Supervisor Evaluations

I would now like to direct my remarks specifically to administrators. If you happen to be in a position in your employment to either give or receive performance reviews, or if you are a leader with the responsibility of training and overseeing other leaders or teachers, you may be able to learn from my experience.

It was standard procedure for an institute teacher to receive two types of evaluations per year. One type of evaluation involved an administrator observing an actual class followed by a private evaluation with the teacher. One time when my teaching was being evaluated, the class went extremely well. The lesson included an enthusiastic and enlightening class discussion. The Spirit was very strong. By the end of the class, I felt like we were all glowing. After class, the administrator started his evaluation by chastising me for not having a "readiness activity" at the beginning of the class. I asked him if the class acted like they needed a readiness activity. He answered that they did not seem to need one but that I should have done one anyway. He seemed to think that his job was to point out negative things and admonish the teacher to improve. The problem was that he could not actually identify any negatives, so he was grasping at straws. He observed that there were 20 students in the class, but only 14 of them had participated in the discussion. I had to do better than that. I told him that the other six were shy and that they would probably stop coming to class if they were pressured to speak out. He insisted that I needed to push them into participation. At the beginning of this evaluation I was euphoric. Then I was surprised, then angry, and then disgusted. However, he was a good man just trying to do his job and I ended up just feeling sorry for him.

Over the years, I was blessed to work with many good leaders and administrators, for which I am very thankful. Sadly, I also observed many teachers being undermined and discouraged by administrators who did not follow Jesus' example of serving with love, receiving feedback, and making adaptations. Instead they tried to do the Lord's work through negative criticism and micro-management.

Jesus had this to say about that management style:

> Ye know that they which are accounted to rule over the Gentiles exercise lordship over them; and their great ones exercise authority upon them. But so shall it not be among you: but whosoever will be great among you, shall be your minister: And whosoever of you will be the chiefest, shall be servant of all. For even the Son of Man came not to be ministered unto, but to minister, and to give his life a ransom for many. (Mark 10:42-45)

The primary responsibility of an administrator is to serve the teacher. Some of the best ways to serve a teacher are: lifting morale, increasing confidence, healing hidden wounds, building trust, and avoiding over-direction.

Some administrators mistakenly think their job is to control the teacher and the teaching methods. It is very easy for this approach to cross the line into Satan's territory of unrighteous dominion. Control does not build better teachers. Administrators would do well to remember,

> No power or influence can or ought to be maintained by virtue of [an administrative position], only by persuasion, by long-suffering, by gentleness and meekness, and by love unfeigned; by kindness, and pure knowledge, which shall greatly enlarge the soul without hypocrisy, and without guile—reproving betimes with sharpness, when moved upon by the Holy Ghost; and then showing forth

afterwards an increase of love toward him whom thou hast reproved, lest he esteem thee to be his enemy; that he may know that thy faithfulness is stronger than the cords of death. (D&C 121:41-44)

Yes, sometimes teachers need reproof. We learn from these verses that such reproof must only happen under the guidance of the Holy Ghost. Evaluators should ask themselves, "Is this teacher truly being negligent, or are they trying to follow the Lord's example in adapting their lesson to their students' needs?"

Student Evaluations

The second type of evaluation that occurred each year was one where the students evaluated the teacher by answering a questionnaire. Over a period of years, a certain student evaluation was being used which stressed specific teaching methods. I usually scored very high except on one question concerning a method which I seldom used. After an administrator admonished me for having a lower score in that area, I made a point to use that method once in the week prior to future evaluations. On those days the quality of the class was diminished, but the scores on that question shot up to match the rest. This type of evaluation did not help me become a more effective teacher.

Student evaluations of teachers are more helpful if given by the teacher and include questions like the following: How do you feel about your class? How do you feel about your teacher? How do you feel about yourself? What have you learned in this class and how will you apply it? How do you think you can help improve your class? Generally speaking, the teacher and class will improve as a result of this kind of evaluation. Of course this kind of evaluation should not be "scored" and should be used to improve teaching rather than as an administrative device.

Evaluating Supervisors

In most educational, business, and political systems, the ones who seem to need it the most seldom solicit or receive evaluation. It is a great tragedy that many leaders and administrators avoid the feedback and evaluation which would help heal them and those they lead. Why? Do they think they are so wise, inspired, or experienced that they do not need to consider feedback, compassion, and adaptation? If so, they need to seek a deeper understanding of what the Lord, who actually is omniscient, has clearly said and demonstrated.

Every administrator would benefit from being evaluated by those who serve under him. That evaluation should include questions like: "How does your supervisor make you feel? Does your manager solicit feedback and make adjustments and improvements? What is your leader doing to help you achieve your highest potential?"

Conclusion

Those who truly desire to follow Jesus need to understand and apply the divine principle of adaptation.

Study or Discussion Questions

1. What have you learned from this analysis of how Jesus leads and teaches?
2. Can you explain the divine principle of adaption and how it applies to you?
3. How are you going to avoid trying to do the Lord's work the devil's way?
4. Why and how are you going to solicit evaluations, and adapt and improve from what you learn?

CHAPTER 28

How Great Shall Be Your Joy

"And if it so be that you should labor all your days in crying repentance unto this people, and bring, save it be one soul unto me, how great shall be your joy with him in the kingdom of my Father!"
(Doctrine and Covenants 18:15)

When I graduated from Weber State College in 1972, I started my career with the Church Educational System (CES) teaching seminary at Bonneville High School in South Ogden, Utah. I taught at Bonneville High Seminary for five years. Then we were asked by CES to transfer to the Paris, Idaho Junior High Seminary, starting the 1977–1978 school year. We lived in Bridgerland Village, Utah on the mountainside overlooking Garden City and stunningly beautiful Bear Lake.

My years at the Bonneville seminary had been happy ones. For the most part, I enjoyed my classes, interacting with other teachers, and working with the student officers. At the Paris Seminary, I was the only teacher and all the students were younger: in the ninth grade. It was somewhat difficult switching from teaching eleventh-graders to ninth-graders. I had to do things differently because of their lower maturity level. Teaching younger students was harder for me, but I knew that

I might have the chance to make a bigger difference by helping students who were younger.

I had heard some good things about the Paris Seminary, and other things that were a bit troubling. Many of the students were descendants of the original pioneers in that area. Many really good people lived there. I had heard that some of the kids in the seminary class had been taking advantage of the previous seminary teacher because he was older and he couldn't see very well. I heard that sometimes when he'd turn to write on the chalkboard, some of the kids would jump out the window without him noticing. Then they would run around the building and the next time he turned around they'd run back into the class and sit down in their seats without him being aware of what was happening. I was upset to hear of this ongoing game.

One day, near the beginning of the school year, I turned to write something on the blackboard and as I turned back, I saw some feet go out the window. I noticed that two of the boys who had been sitting in the row of seats by the window were missing. It was a first floor window and there was a grassy hill about three feet below the window. I just kept talking as if I had noticed nothing, even though there were a few giggles. A few minutes later, I turned to write on the board again and when I turned around, those two young men were back in their seats, chuckling.

I continued talking as if nothing had happened and began walking back and forth in front of the room. Then I walked over to the aisle next to the window. One of the boys who had gone out the window was very small in stature and the other was one of the biggest, toughest boys in the school. He was also an outstanding athlete.

I just kept talking normally and moved around the room until I was standing next to the larger student and then, right in mid-sentence, I reached out and picked him up out of his chair and threw him headfirst out the window. Immediately, I turned back to the smaller student and threw him out the window too. After that, I leaned out the window and said very loudly, "There's only one way people in my class ever go out the window and that's if I throw them out! Now, you boys get back in here and sit down." Just a few seconds later those two boys hustled back in the room and sat down in their seats. I smiled at them and continued the lesson. Everything went normally after that.

Later that day, another student approached me before class. "Will you please throw me out the window during class?"

"Why would you ask me that?"

"Well, you know, it's all over the school what happened and everybody thinks it's so cool and so if you'd throw me out the window like you did the other guys then everyone would think I was cool too."

I laughed and told him that I did not plan to throw anyone else out the window. The two boys that I threw out the window soon became my friends. I liked them. They liked me. We had a mutual understanding and respect for each other. Later, I remembered that my wife's grandpa, David Eskelson, told a story about throwing one of his students out the window, which also ended well. Of course, nowadays, a teacher would get fired and sued over something like that. But in that day and time everything worked out well for all of us.

Overall, that year was a good one. One very special thing we did that year was to arrange for the seminary to sponsor a concert by Marvin Payne. We invited him to have dinner at our home. Also attending that dinner were two outstanding student leaders from the Paris Seminary: Shelly Daines and Charlotte Smart. All of the Paris Seminary students were invited to attend the concert. Some seminary student leaders from the

Bonneville Seminary in Ogden, Utah also attended. The concert was held at the Sweet Water Resort on the south shore of Bear Lake. Everyone seemed to have a wonderful time. Thirty-seven years later, Shelly remembered the details and inspiration of that evening.

After that year, they closed down the Paris Junior High School and bussed the kids to Montpelier, Idaho. Four years later, when that group of ninth-graders were graduating from high school and seminary, some of the student leaders contacted me in Farmington, Utah and asked me if I'd come to Montpelier for their seminary graduation. I was surprised, but I told them that I'd be happy to come. Barbra and I went up to the seminary graduation and were treated as "honored guests." It was almost embarrassing how much attention we received and how many wonderful things were said to us. We were surrounded by so many students who expressed their love and appreciation for the experience that we'd had together in the Paris Junior High Seminary. It was amazing to be there, to share in their graduation and to see how they had grown and matured into wonderful people.

In 2003, when I was teaching institute in Missouri, CES asked if I'd be willing to teach at a large Institute of Religion in Utah. We were surprised, but happy to accept the assignment. Not long after we moved back to Utah, my wife and I went out to eat at a Mexican restaurant. As we were sitting at a table a woman who was quite a bit younger than us rushed up to me, took me by the hands, lifted me up out of the chair and began to hug me and cry. I didn't recognize her and couldn't figure out who she was. But she kept crying and hugging me as she said over and over, "You saved my life! You saved my life!"

After a while she calmed down enough to quit crying. "You remember me, don't you?"

"I'm sorry, I don't remember you."

"I understand. It's been a long time. I had a twin sister. We were in your class at Paris, Idaho. We used to come and spend a lot of time after school in your office talking to you. We used to lay on the floor in your office and cry and cry and cry."

The memories came flooding back. They had some serious problems at home and were having a hard time coping. I spent a lot of time trying to help them feel better. I tried to help them recognize and receive the blessings of the gospel, in spite of their difficult circumstances. After I remembered everything, I was in tears too. A few minutes later she explained that she had made a lot of good decisions in her life and that she had been very blessed. She was grateful for the help that I had given her and truly felt like I had saved her life. For many years she had no idea how to get in touch with me, so she was grateful to finally have a chance to see me and tell me how she felt. I was grateful too.

Over the years, there were many students who were very kind and appreciative of my efforts as a teacher. There have also been a few students who openly disliked me. I have found that it is best not to take any praise or criticism too seriously. Most of the time you do not know how students really feel and how things will turn out for them. It's a wonderful and rewarding thing to have positive experiences with former students and friends.

Recently, we went to visit one of our sons in Arizona. While we were in church, he told me that there was a sister in his ward who knew me from when I taught seminary and institute years before in New Mexico. At the end of the class, he found her and brought us together in the hallway. As soon as she saw me, she threw her arms around me and began to cry. I remembered her well and hugged her back. It was an emotional time for both of us. My family lived in New Mexico between 1984 and 1990 while I served as a seminary and institute teacher. I also served as the local CES coordinator and supervised several early morning seminary teachers. Because of the heavy workload, I was authorized to have a secretary in that area and there were several wonderful sisters who served under my direction.

This particular sister was an excellent secretary, even though she was dealing with some difficulties in her personal life. I was asked by the LDS Social Services to counsel with several people in that area, including her. I was able to help her deal with some of the problems in her life. Not long after that, she moved and got another job. I always wondered how things had turned out for her. As we stood there in the hallway of the church, crying and hugging each other, she said over and over, "You saved my life! You saved my life!" We had a very pleasant talk and it was obvious that she was doing very well. When my son and I left the church and went out to his car I was overcome with emotion and cried tears of happiness for quite a while.

I'm very grateful for the experiences I have described here and others like them. Teachers do not have the satisfaction of knowing what happens to most of their students. Occasionally those opportunities do come and when lives have turned out well, it is deeply gratifying for the teacher to have had some small part in that success.

Lesson Insight

"But lay up for yourselves treasures in heaven, where neither moth nor rust doth corrupt, and where thieves do not break through nor steal." (3 Nephi 13:20) What exactly are the treasures in heaven that we are to lay up? Here are a few verses about what the Lord thinks of as his treasures. "For the LORD hath chosen Jacob unto himself, and Israel for his peculiar treasure." (Psalms 135:4) "Now therefore, if ye will obey my voice indeed, and keep my covenant, then ye shall be a peculiar treasure unto me above all people." (Exodus 19:5) According the Bible Dictionary, peculiar means, "one's very own, exclusive, or special." Peculiar is "not used in the Bible as odd or eccentric." We are the Lord's treasures. His purpose is to "lay up" or bring to heaven a covenant people. We are also commanded to lay up for ourselves treasures in heaven. Our treasures will also be people: those we have loved, shared the gospel with, and labored in behalf of through family history and temple work. I envision a reunion similar to the City of Enoch's, where "we will receive them into our bosom, and they shall see us; and we will fall upon their necks, and they shall fall upon our necks, and we will kiss each other." (Moses 7:63)

Homework

1. Who are your "treasures"? Make a list. Express your love and appreciation to them.

2. Pretend you are one of your deceased ancestors who is waiting for their family history and temple work to be done. Write a letter to your descendants.

3. Make a list of people who have had a positive influence on your life. Find a way to express your gratitude to some of them.

CHAPTER 29
The Doctrine of Boundaries

"And unto every kingdom is given a law; and unto every law there are certain bounds also and conditions." (D&C 88:39)

The importance of obedience has been well established. However, the Lord is not in the business of creating automatons or robots. He wants his sons and daughters to become kings and queens. Carefully consider the following quotes:

> For behold, it is not meet that I should command in all things; for he that is compelled in all things, the same is a slothful and not a wise servant; wherefore he receiveth no reward. Verily I say, men should be anxiously engaged in a good cause, and do many things of their own free will, and bring to pass much righteousness; For the power is in them, wherein they are agents unto themselves. And inasmuch as men do good they shall in nowise lose their reward. But he that doeth not anything until he is commanded, and receiveth a commandment with doubtful heart, and keepeth it with slothfulness, the same is damned. (D&C 58:26-29)

> Now those men, or those women, who know no more about the power of God, and the influences of the Holy Spirit, than to be led entirely by another person, suspending their own understanding, and pinning their faith upon

another's sleeve, will never be capable of entering into the celestial glory, to be crowned as they anticipate; they will never be capable of becoming Gods. They cannot rule themselves, to say nothing of ruling others, but they must be dictated to in every trifle, like a child. They cannot control themselves in the least, but James, Peter, or somebody else must control them. They never can become Gods, nor be crowned as rulers with glory, immortality, and eternal lives. They never can hold scepters of glory, majesty, and power in the celestial kingdom. Who will? Those who are valiant and inspired with the true independence of heaven, who will go forth boldly in the service of their God, leaving others to do as they please, determined to do right, though all mankind besides should take the opposite course. (Brigham Young, *The Best of Joseph and Brigham*, GVS, 161)

When combined, the quotes above, and many similar ones, seem to result in an impossible paradox. How can we be completely obedient and creatively independent at the same time?

Happily, the Lord has revealed the solution.

And again, verily I say unto you, that which is governed by law is also preserved by law and perfected and sanctified by the same ... And there are many kingdoms ... And unto every kingdom is given a law; and unto every law there are certain bounds also and conditions. All beings who abide not in those conditions are not justified. (D&C 88:34-39)

There are many different kinds of boundaries. Some are personal. Most of us become uncomfortable if someone invades our personal or emotional space. Some are geographical, such as property lines and national borders. Some boundaries help establish identity and meaning. There have been good books written about boundary management in business, psychology, and marriage. Some boundaries are closely connected with values, as explained in the following quote.

Rather than telling us everything we must do, or compelling in all things, The Ten Commandments establish boundaries of beneficial behavior. Clear boundaries are the beginning of autonomy and freedom. Instead of rebelling about "thou shalt not's", we should recognize that these laws are blessings which promote our happiness by helping us not to harm and preventing us from being harmed. Behaviors outside these boundaries are to be avoided because they are destructive. Within these boundaries we are free to choose and enjoy an infinite range of creative and desirable activities. This is the brilliance of The Ten Commandments: they plainly state the outside boundaries of acceptable behavior, while allowing tremendous autonomy inside those bounds. (GVS, *Pillars of Truth and Freedom*, 12)

Thus we see that good boundaries help to reconcile the impossible by restricting evil and promoting independence at the same time. Amazingly, boundaries actually promote creativity and empowerment within doctrinal and organizational hierarchy.

Here is a simple example to start you thinking about how all of this might apply to you. Many years ago, soon after one of my sons married, I noticed that he and his wife were having frequent conflicts. I watched and listened for quite a while, hoping to find a way to help them without being intrusive. At the right time, I initiated a discussion with them. I told them what I had observed and they agreed that my observations were correct. Figuratively speaking, they were stomping on each other's toes, resulting in a lot of conflict. I told them that I thought they were both great people with good intentions. Then I told them that most of their hurt feelings and conflicts had to do with boundaries. They had no idea what I was talking about, so I explained the doctrine of boundaries as given above.

Then we all discussed what boundaries might be helpful in their relationship. In doing so, we agreed that food decisions and preparation methods were her domain. Camping gear was his domain. We then agreed that they would avoid crossing the boundaries into each other's domains. Additionally, we went through half a dozen other things and agreed on boundaries. I committed them to keep discussing and agreeing on boundary issues. Since no one is perfect, I encouraged them to respond to boundary intrusions with a smile and the single word "Boundaries." They each agreed to back off from any boundary violation.

They implemented my "boundary counsel." Almost immediately, their conflict declined dramatically. And guess what else? They both made significant advancements within their established boundaries. They were much happier. A few months later, my daughter-in-law expressed appreciation to me with hugs and tears for helping them to improve their marriage.

Discussion Questions

1. What do you think about the paradox between obedience and creative independence?
2. How can you apply the principles taught in this chapter to your life?

CHAPTER 30

Beyond the Mark

"Wherefore, because of their blindness, which blindness came by looking beyond the mark, they must needs fall..." (Jacob 4:14)

Going beyond the mark is a plague that infects churches, government, business, education, and families. In business, the practice of going beyond the mark often shows up in the form of micromanagement. A review of micromanagement from a business standpoint generates the following highlights: (1) Micromanagement goes beyond what is necessary and is usually a form of mismanagement. (2) Micromanagement stifles employee development, potential, and creativity. (3) Under micromanagement there is a decrease in quality, quantity, effectiveness, and efficiency. (4) Micromanagement increases employee dissatisfaction and workforce turnover. (5) Micromanagers are usually in denial concerning their tactics and the negative consequences.

In contrast, God's purpose is to enable those who follow him to achieve their highest potential.

> And the Lord God spake unto Moses, saying: The heavens, they are many, and they cannot be numbered unto man; but they are numbered unto me, for they are mine. And as one earth shall pass away, and the heavens thereof even so shall another come; and there is no end

to my works, neither to my words. For behold, this is my work and my glory—to bring to pass the immortality and eternal life of man. (Moses 1:37-39)

Observe the difference between God's plan and Satan's in the following verses.

And I, the Lord God, spake unto Moses, saying: That Satan, whom thou hast commanded in the name of mine Only Begotten, is the same which was from the beginning, and he came before me, saying—Behold, here am I, send me, I will be thy son, and I will redeem all mankind, that one soul shall not be lost, and surely I will do it; wherefore give me thine honor. But, behold, my Beloved Son, which was my Beloved and Chosen from the beginning, said unto me—Father, thy will be done, and the glory be thine forever. Wherefore, because that Satan rebelled against me, and sought to destroy the agency of man, which I, the Lord God, had given him, and also, that I should give unto him mine own power; by the power of mine Only Begotten, I caused that he should be cast down; And he became Satan, yea, even the devil, the father of all lies, to deceive and to blind men, and to lead them captive at his will, even as many as would not hearken unto my voice. (Moses 4:1-4)

Wherefore, men are free according to the flesh; and all things are given them which are expedient unto man. And they are free to choose liberty and eternal life, through the great Mediator of all men, or to choose captivity and death, according to the captivity and power of the devil; for he seeketh that all men might be miserable like unto himself. (2 Nephi 2:27)

In his mortal ministry Jesus gave the following instruction,

Then spake Jesus to the multitude, and to his disciples, saying, The Scribes and the Pharisees sit in Moses' seat. All, therefore, whatsoever they bid you observe, they will make you observe and do… But do not ye after their works; for they say, and do not. For they bind heavy burdens and lay on men's shoulders, and they are grievous to be borne; but they will not move them with one of their fingers. (JST Matthew 23:1-3, full version)

But he that is greatest among you shall be your servant. And whosoever shall exalt himself shall be abased; and he that shall humble himself shall be exalted ... Woe unto you, scribes and Pharisees, hypocrites! for ye pay tithe of mint and anise and cummin, and have omitted the weightier matters of the law, judgment, mercy, and faith: these ought ye to have done, and not to leave the other undone. Ye blind guides, which strain at a gnat, and swallow a camel. (Matthew 23:11-12, 23-24)

We will conclude the scriptural insight section of this lesson with the crowning instruction of this dispensation pertaining to going beyond the mark.

Behold, there are many called, but few are chosen. And why are they not chosen? Because their hearts are set so much upon the things of this world, and aspire to the honors of men, that they do not learn this one lesson—That the rights of the priesthood are inseparably connected with the powers of heaven, and that the powers of heaven cannot be controlled nor handled only upon the principles of righteousness. That they may be conferred upon us, it is true; but when we undertake to cover our sins, or to gratify our pride, our vain ambition, or to exercise control or dominion or compulsion upon the souls of the children of men, in any degree of unrighteousness, behold, the heavens withdraw themselves; the Spirit of the Lord is grieved; and when it is withdrawn, Amen to the priesthood or the authority of that man ... We have learned by sad experience that it is the nature and disposition of almost all men, as soon as they get a little authority, as they suppose, they will immediately begin to exercise unrighteous dominion. Hence many are called, but few are chosen. No power or influence can or ought to be maintained by virtue of the priesthood, only by persuasion, by long-suffering, by gentleness and meekness, and by love unfeigned ... and thy scepter an unchanging scepter of righteousness and truth; and thy dominion shall be an everlasting dominion, and without compulsory means it shall flow unto thee forever and ever. (D&C 121:34-37, 39-41, 46)

Hugh Nibley connected the concept of "looking beyond the mark" with the phrase "zeal without knowledge." He compared some church members in the last days to those of old who

> looked beyond the mark ... giving their young people and old awards for zeal alone, zeal without knowledge— for sitting in endless meetings, for dedicated conformity, and unlimited capacity for suffering boredom. We think it is more commendable to get up at 5:00 a.m ... to write a bad book than to get up at nine o'clock to write a good one—that is pure zeal that tends to breed a race of insufferable, self-righteous prigs with barren minds. (Hugh Nibley, *On the Timely and the Timeless: Zeal Without Knowledge*, 270-271)

I have associated with a few zealous leaders who go beyond the mark in their callings: micromanaging when they should be supporting, and demanding "endless meetings" and "dedicated conformity" from those whom they have been called to love and serve. Consider the following examples:

Many years ago I was called to be the Sunday School *Gospel Doctrine* class teacher. Our large class met in the chapel. I taught from the pulpit, using the mic, so that everyone could hear well. We had good class discussions. Brother Redd, the Sunday School superintendent, wanted the class to sit together in a tight group at the front of the chapel. I told him I disagreed because their attendance and comfort were more important to me than where they sat. He insisted that I make the announcement. The next week at the beginning of the class, I obediently announced that Brother Redd had instructed me to tell the class that he wanted them to sit together in a tight group at the front. The next week they sat in their usual spread-out, comfortable places and we had an excellent class. After class, Brother Redd was very angry that they had not followed his instruction.

I again served as the *Gospel Doctrine* class teacher in a different ward, and again, the class was being held in the chapel. Several people with hearing issues liked it there so that they could use earphones to tie into the sound system. It was announced that everyone needed to sit together in the middle section in the front. I was not consulted and did not say anything to anyone about it. People who had babies and special needs continued to sit farther back. Soon it was decided that the class would be moved into the Relief Society room so that everyone would be forced to sit close, even though it should have been obvious that the room was not big enough. As soon as the move took place, class attendance dropped off by about a third. Among those not attending were the ones with babies and those with special needs. It went on like that for about a month. When the class was moved back to the chapel, class members were allowed to sit where they wanted, and attendance went back up.

When I was serving as a stake high councilor in a Missouri-based stake, I was assigned to speak in a ward in Arkansas. Large, intimidating ushers stood at the chapel doors during the administration of the sacrament. No one was allowed to leave for any reason: not if they were sick, not for a trip to the bathroom, not with a crying baby. Even though their intentions were good, some leaders had clearly gone beyond the mark.

This is what the war in heaven was all about: Satan did not say that he was going to force the people to be bad. He said that he was going to force them to be good by establishing excessive controls. The Lord has stated that almost all people, "as soon as they get a little authority, as they suppose, they will immediately begin to exercise unrighteous dominion" which grieves the Spirit of the Lord and causes him to withdraw. (D&C 121:39) In other words, chances are good that we have all been guilty of unrighteous dominion from time to time. Every one of us needs to think about what ethics and values we adhere to in administering our department, family, or calling. Freedom (agency) is a top priority with the Lord and with those who truly follow him. If our leadership does not help those we supervise to reach their highest potential, and to be happy and prosperous along the way, we might be trying to do the Lord's work the devil's way. By this, I do not mean that we are bad people who are intentionally choosing evil. In most cases we are good people trying to do the right thing, but going about it the wrong way. Good, active people sincerely trying to do the Lord's work using Lucifer's methods, because it is "the best way they know," generally have no idea how much harm they are doing to themselves and others.

Some might be tempted to think that their position allows them to go beyond the mark. They need to think again. Even the prophet does not go beyond the bounds the Lord sets. God himself does not go beyond the established bounds, or he "would cease to be God." (Alma 42:22-26) So no matter how sure you are that you are right or inspired, you are not authorized to implement procedures, programs, reports, or rules that have not been firmly established though the proper line of authority. To do so goes beyond the mark and puts you on unholy ground where you "must needs fall."

In contrast, Christlike leaders who carefully avoid going beyond the mark bring out the best in those they supervise. Many years ago I was supervised by a CES area director named Richard Arnold. He always treated those who worked under his direction with patience and kindness. I could tell that he loved me and wanted to help me reach my full potential. I was always anxious and happy to do whatever he asked and help him with anything he needed to the best of my ability. I have been blessed to work with many leaders like him and have tried to follow their examples.

Discussion Questions

1. In what ways do you have a tendency to be a micromanager or go beyond the mark?
2. Why is going beyond the mark such a big problem?
3. What are you going to do to avoid being a micromanager or going beyond the mark?
4. What principles of good leadership related to this chapter are you going to follow?

CHAPTER 31

Defending Yourself, Others, and the Truth

"Yea, and he was a man who was firm in the faith of Christ, and he had sworn with an oath to defend his people, his rights, and his country, and his religion, even to the loss of his blood. Now the Nephites were taught to defend themselves against their enemies, even to the shedding of blood if it were necessary; yea, and they were also taught never to give an offense, yea, and never to raise the sword except it were against an enemy, except it were to preserve their lives." (Alma 48:13-14)

Most institute faculty meetings that I have attended over the years were productive, informative, and uplifting. However, I would like to discuss two meetings that were somewhat atypical in nature.

One day, an author, whom I will call Larry, made a presentation to our institute faculty. He had done many years of research related to the Book of Mormon and was the author of a very interesting book. After his presentation, I bought his book and read it, and he and I had some congenial discussions and correspondence. As of this writing, the book does not seem to be in print any longer, as is common with scholarly books.

In his book, Larry referred to an account in a different book titled, *Moroni: American Prophet, Modern Messenger* by H. Donl

Peterson. In that book, on page 72, Brother Peterson quotes an account originally dating from 1896 which says, "In answer to prayer the Lord gave Joseph a vision, in which appeared a wild country and on the scene was Moroni after whom were six Indians [Lamanites ?] in pursuit; he stopped and one of the Indians stepped forward and measured swords with him. Moroni smote him and he fell dead; another Indian advanced and contended with him; this Indian also fell by his sword; a third Indian then stepped forth and met the same fate; a fourth afterwards contended with him, but in the struggle with the fourth, Moroni being exhausted, was killed." Donl Peterson estimated that Moroni would have been at least 70 years old at the time.

In his own book, Larry states that he did not believe this account because it seemed out of character for Moroni to kill three Lamanites under these circumstances. I later brought this up in a face to face discussion with Larry at the institute.

He reasserted his belief. "Moroni would not have killed those men because he had already buried the plates, seen the future, loved his Lamanite brethren, and was a man of peace."

I expressed my opinion. "Moroni would have killed them, acting on the correct principle of self-defense."

"If I was Moroni, I would not have killed anyone to save my own life."

I responded, "I would have dispatched them because they were obviously murderers. I would be justified in acting in self-defense, and I would also be saving all their future victims. In a mortal world people die. The real issue is whether those who die will be the guilty or the innocent. How could you live with your conscience knowing that the murderer's future victims would die because of your failure to protect them?"

"That is not my responsibility."

"That is where you and I are different because I feel responsible to help protect others."

"But what about the people of Ammon? They didn't fight."

"The Ammonites were a special case. But remember that they sent their sons to war and were great supporters of the war effort. Those sons were led in battle by Helaman, who was the chief high priest and leader of the church. Without their participation, the Nephites would have lost major battles and many lives. I greatly appreciate your excellent research and insights. I am also concerned that your book seems to be tainted by pacifism."

Eventually, we agreed to disagree and parted on friendly terms. Sometimes self-defense requires defending yourself or others even unto death. This is a righteous principle, as demonstrated by Moroni and many others in the Book of Mormon.

At another faculty meeting, a presentation was to be made by a man who was promoting what he believed to be an actual photograph of Joseph Smith. I was able to view this photo prior to the meeting and was not impressed. It made Joseph look like a weakling. I was not going to let that go unchallenged. I happen to own a replica of the death mask of Joseph Smith, which is an exact image of his face. Before anyone entered the meeting room where the presentation was to take place, I put the mounted death mask on a table at the front of the room.

When the time came, we all gathered for the meeting. The replica death mask remained in place throughout the meeting. The presenter gave an excellent and convincing presentation, asserting that the picture was an actual photograph of Joseph Smith. He made no mention of the death mask that was sitting there in plain sight and no one else said anything about it either. However, I do not think his presentation had the desired effect because the photograph he promoted clearly looked nothing like Joseph's death mask.

After the meeting was over and everyone had left the room, I retrieved the death mask and took it back home, where it is displayed in a prominent place. It is a constant reminder that Joseph sealed his testimony with his blood. Even though Joseph had prophesied that he would be martyred, he tried to defend himself and his brethren by firing shots into the mob. Acting on the same correct principle, Moroni would have defended himself and others with the sword.

It is important to stand against what is not true, and it is just as important to present and explain the truth. It should be done tactfully if possible. Notice that I avoided saying anything in the meetings, which would be embarrassing to either presenter, while at the same time, my efforts probably had some corrective effect. If you love and respect someone, like I do Moroni and Joseph, then you defend them, as I did Moroni and Joseph.

Discussion Questions

1. What is the correct principle of self-defense?
2. To what extent, and with what weapons, are you prepared to defend yourself and others?
3. How do you feel about the way I defended Moroni and Joseph? Can you suggest some better ways of handling similar situations?

CHAPTER 32
Swift Witness

"And I will come near to you to judgment; and I will be a swift witness against… those that oppress the hireling in his wages… and fear not me, saith the LORD of hosts." (Malachi 3:5)

During the last few years that I served as a teacher at the Institute of Religion, our institute was picked to be part of a pilot program for a new computer program which was intended to handle student records including registration, attendance, credit and grades. Since the computer program at first seemed to take a "penny wise and pound foolish" approach, I will refer to it as PPF.

A faculty meeting was held to introduce the program to the local administration and teachers. After a long presentation they asked if there were any questions or comments. After a few people parroted positive comments I raised my hand. "With all due respect, it is obvious that PPF will not work as expected. These processes are too difficult for the students, teachers, and staff. I think PPF should be replaced or simplified by outside contractors who would guarantee its effectiveness." My concerns were belittled and dismissed.

When we started to use the program there were huge problems, beginning with student registration. Many students just gave up because of the difficulty and bugs in the program. Then the faculty and staff had to spend countless extra hours processing incomplete registrations. However, we all did the best we could with what we had and many improvements were eventually made to the PPF program.

Each teacher was responsible to enter class attendance, grades, etc. into the program. It was not long before I was helping several teachers with their records. Some of the secretarial staff were doing the same thing for other teachers.

After more than a semester of struggling with the program I wrote the following letter to the administration and requested that it be passed up the line.

Dear Brother Brown, (names changed)

As we discussed, I have conducted an informal survey of a few teachers to determine how many hours are being spent working with PPF. Each of the these teachers does all PPF related work himself without using support staff.

Average hours per week spent during the first four weeks of this semester:

Brother Red	4 hours
Brother Blue	4 hours
Brother Green	7 hours
Brother Black	3 hours
Brother Yellow	4 hours
Total:	22 hours
Average per teacher:	4.4 hours per week

Time spent accomplishing those tasks with the previous system was less than one hour per week. Thus, there has been about a 350% increase in average time spent per teacher per week.

If the average teacher is making about $52,000 per year then he makes about $25 per hour. Based on an average increase of 3.5 hours per week, the net cost in wages for using PPF comes to about $87 per teacher per week. If school is taught 36 weeks per year the increased cost is about $3,132 per teacher per year. **That means that the average cost of PPF per 1000 teachers would be $3,132,000 per year. If there were 2,700 teachers using PPF at these rates, the cost would come to $8,456,400 per year.** Note that this figure does not include increased time spent by support staff at any level.

Even more important than the monetary loss, is the loss of teacher time available for students, lesson preparation, and related enrollment and completion efforts. The above figures relating to PPF may only represent the "tip of the iceberg" relating to leadership challenges.

A few months after I submitted this letter, changes were made to the PPF program and process that reduced teacher time per week to about one hour. I often wondered if I helped save over eight million dollars worth of labor per year. If the program creators had solicited feedback from front line users before implementing the program, much frustration and wasted time could have been avoided.

Technically speaking, the money paid to those teachers was not totally lost, but the time and effort they were being paid for was diverted. What was lost during that diversion? Did class preparation and teaching suffer, were students neglected, did attendance and completion drop? Measuring the misuse of time and effort is more difficult than accounting for funds.

In business accounting, the cost of a project must include the "cost of labor" or "labor expenses." Costs which exclude labor expenses would usually be considered misleading and inaccurate. Not including labor when calculating costs could be considered deceptive. However, it appears that many projects have been approved without reference to the cost of labor involved.

This is a serious budgeting issue, but avoiding exploitation of the laborer is actually a doctrinal imperative. Brigham Young said,

> Labor builds our meeting houses, temples, court houses, fine halls for music and fine school houses; it is labor that teaches our children, and makes them acquainted with the various branches of education... Time and ability to labor are the capital stock of the whole world of mankind, and we are all indebted to God for the ability to use time to advantage, and he will require of us a strict account of the disposition we make of this ability; and he will not only require an account of our acts, but our words and thoughts will also be brought into judgment. (*Teachings of the Presidents of the Church: Brigham Young*, 228-229)

I once heard of an administrator who bragged that he had saved funds by keeping wages low. Apparently he failed to consider what Jesus said concerning the Second Coming,

> And I will come near to you to judgment; and I will be a swift witness against the sorcerers, and against the adulterers, and against false swearers, and against those that oppress the hireling in his wages, the widow, and the fatherless, and that turn aside the stranger from his right, and fear not me, saith the LORD of hosts. (Malachi 3:5; 3 Nephi 24:5. See also Leviticus 19:13; Deuteronomy 24:14, 15; James 5:4)

One of the primary things Christ will judge people harshly for is devaluing people and their work. Ever since I began to consider the possibility of Jesus being a swift witness against me rather than my advocate I have been very careful to avoid anything that might be associated with oppressing the hireling in his time or wages.

Study and Discussion Questions

1. Why do you suppose my concerns about the new computer program were belittled and dismissed?

2. Why might the letter I wrote have been effective?

3. How do you feel about failure to consider labor costs in expenditure proposals for family, business, church, or government?

4. What is the connection between the doctrine of labor expressed by Brigham Young and the Lord's judgement against oppressive employers?

5. What are you willing to do in order to avoid "oppressing the hireling" in his/her time or wages?

CHAPTER 33
Greater Love Than Mine

"Behold, what manner of love the Father hath bestowed upon us..."
(1 John 3:1)

"For I am persuaded, that neither death, nor life, nor angels, nor principalities, nor powers, nor things present, nor things to come, Nor height, nor depth, nor any other creature, shall be able to separate us from the love of God, which is in Christ Jesus our Lord."
(Romans 8:38-39)

When we lived in Providence, Utah, one of our sons came back to live with us. He had been struggling with a very difficult marriage for many years. Finally, the marriage ended in divorce. We loved our son very much and were happy to be with him, even under these very sad and difficult circumstances.

When he moved home, he was really downtrodden and not the same person who had left our home years before. He had experienced some very dark times. It was heart-wrenching for us to see him that way. He lived with us for about a year and a half while he struggled to heal and start a new life. One of the issues he faced was his social status. When someone is older and divorced with children, they are usually not considered to be the ideal social companion. He was older than most of the single people in our area. He didn't have any family or friends there except us. However, he tried hard to do the right thing, stay active in the church, and to overcome his difficulties. We saw significant positive changes, and as a result, more light came back into his life. Over time, he returned to the happier version of himself that we had always known.

After about a year had passed, he met a wonderful woman and they started dating seriously. Eventually, they decided to get married. They went through all the proper steps to get clearance for a temple marriage. Life was good again for our son. After they had been married for only a few months, they were invited to meet with their Stake President. They thought it would probably be a Stake calling for her, but the Stake President asked if my son would be willing to serve as a counselor in the new bishopric for their ward. His initial reaction was, "You don't even know me."

The stake president replied, "It's true we don't know you, but your new bishop does, and he has requested that you be one of his counselors."

My son was still dumbfounded. "The new bishop and I don't know each other very well."

"Nevertheless, you're the one we'd like to call. Are you worthy and willing to serve as a counselor in your bishopric?"

"Well, yes."

Shortly thereafter, he met with the new bishop. He couldn't help but ask, "You know, we don't know each other very well. Why did you call me to be your counselor?"

The bishop answered, "I was in the temple praying about whom my counselors should be and the Lord spoke very clearly to me that you were to be one of them. I am grateful that you're willing to serve."

Not long after that, my son called me. "Will you come down and ordain me to be a high priest before they set me apart as our new bishop's counselor?"

I was wonderfully surprised by these events and said that I would be happy to do that. My son went on to make significant contributions in that bishopric. About a year later, I went with him on their ward fathers and sons camp-out. I observed his interactions with the ward members on the outing. It was wonderful to see the relationships that he had with them and the way he helped them.

When I first heard that my son was being called to serve in a bishopric, I thought, "I don't think there is anybody who loves my son more than I do. I don't think there is anyone who understands him and his potential more than I do." I considered my strong feelings of love for him and the relationship we shared. I thought that if I had been asked if he was prepared to serve in a bishopric I would have answered, "Maybe you'd better wait a few years." No sooner did I have that thought than pure knowledge and understanding flowed through me. The Holy Ghost taught me that the Lord loved my son more than I did. He understood him and knew his potential better than I did. I realized at a new depth that my love for my son was not as great or wonderful as Heavenly Father's love for him. I guess that's something that intellectually should be obvious, but I had never really felt and understood it to that depth before. I thought about each of my children, my wife, and all of the other people I loved so much. I realized that the Lord loves them more than I do and He's willing to help them, forgive them, and bless them, even more than I am. I felt very humbled by the vast love that I knew the Lord has for my children and other loved ones. That experience was, and continues to be, life-altering.

Around the same time that I had this epiphany about God's love, I had a good friend who was having some trouble with one of his sons. This father was spending a lot of time on his knees, praying about the situation. He was desperately seeking to know how to help his son, what he should or shouldn't do. He wanted to know what was going to happen, and how things were ever going to work out. He told me that one night when he was praying about his son, the Lord spoke to him very clearly and said, "I loved him before you did. Have faith. Have faith. Have faith. I'll help him through it."

Discussion Questions

1. What lessons of faith and love can we learn by observing how the Lord helps us and our children?
2. How can understanding the depth of the Lord's love help you and your loved ones get through difficult times?

CHAPTER 34

Jesus Walks the Halls of This Prison

"I was in prison and ye came unto me." (Matthew 25:36)

NOTE: This chapter contains elements from several talks talks I was asked to give at the Gunnison, Utah Prison in 2012 and 2014. There were many LDS prisoners at that facility, including some returned missionaries. The church had an excellent and beneficial organization there which included programs, leaders, and missionary couples.

To start with today, I'd like to refer to some things the Savior taught, as recorded in Matthew chapter 25, starting in verse 31. Jesus said,

> When the Son of man shall come in his glory, and all the holy angels with him, then he shall sit upon the throne of his glory: And before him shall be gathered all nations: and he shall separate them one from another, as a shepherd divideth his sheep from the goats: And he shall set the sheep on his right hand, but the goats on his left. Then shall the King say to them on his right hand, Come, ye blessed of my Father, inherit the kingdom prepared for you from the foundation of the world: For I was an hungred, and ye gave me meat: I was thirsty, and ye gave me drink: I was a stranger, and ye took me in: Naked, and ye clothed me: I was sick, and ye visited me: I was in prison, and ye came unto me. Then shall the righteous answer

him, saying, Lord, when saw we thee an hungred, and fed thee? or thirsty, and gave thee drink? When saw we thee a stranger, and took thee in? or naked, and clothed thee? Or when saw we thee sick, or in prison, and came unto thee? And the King shall answer and say unto them, Verily, I say unto you, Inasmuch as ye have done it unto one of the least of these my brethren, ye have done it unto me. (Matthew 25:31-40)

Now think about how that applies to you and me. He said the day of judgment would be better for those who visit and help prisoners. Why would he say that? He said it because loves prisoners. Some of you have many people who love you. Some of you may have only a few who love you. Maybe some of you even feel like there isn't anybody who loves you.

The Church has made sure that there are people here to help you and to love you. We can help and love each other, but none of us can help you or love you as much as the Lord. Jesus said, "I was in prison, and ye came unto me." In other words, the Lord, Jesus Christ, symbolically put himself in your position and said to everyone, "Inasmuch as ye have done it unto one of the least of these my brethren, ye have done it unto me." Always remember that the Lord cares about and loves prisoners, including you.

When I spoke here two years ago, there was a man here who would later become my friend. I didn't meet him or talk with him then. He has since been released and now lives in my area. He does auto mechanics and auto body work. He and his father have a little auto repair business and he has done repair work for me. I see him in church every week and sometimes we go out to eat together. I am happy and grateful that we have become friends.

Last Sunday at church, I asked him if there was anything he would like to say to his brethren who are still in prison here. He responded, "Oh yes! But they won't let me in."

I replied, "I'm going there to give another talk next Friday. If you would like to write something up, I'll incorporate it into my talk." Yesterday, we met for lunch and he gave me some handwritten pages containing things he wanted to say to you. I have added some additional notes about other things that he told me.

These are not my words. They are not things I could or would say. I think you will understand what he says better than I do. It has been suggested that I not use his name, but some of you may be able to figure out who he is. I don't know you very well, but I told him a few of your names and gave him a few descriptions. He recognized some of you.

Here is what he wrote:

> I was asked if I would like to say anything to you gentlemen, from me to you. First of all, it would be, thank you. From 2009 through 2012, I was housed in 'Aspen 1' with ten months in 'Strive.' From 2012–2013, I spent time in the 'Dog Block' in Draper. During my time with many of you, I learned a lot. Those years were some of the best years of my life. Here are some of the things that I learned that are very important to my life.
>
> 1. Be honest. Tell the truth always and be willing to take the heat, even if you don't agree.
> 2. You are entitled to nothing. Anything worth having is worth earning, including respect.
> 3. Don't blame others for how you feel, for where you are, or for your choices. You are the only person who can represent who you are.
> 4. When you think that you are out of options, remember that there is always another choice.
> 5. Always carry an attitude of gratitude. It is much worse in other places.

6. Life is not easier out here. It can be hateful and depressing and full of anger and fear. It can also be wonderful and exciting and fun. Out here, as much as in there, it is how you choose to let life affect you that is most important.

Believe it or not, there are some scriptures that assist me as much now as they did then, and both of them are about being who you can be. The first one is in 2 Nephi 1:21 where father Lehi says, 'Arise from the dust, my sons, and be men.' The next one is from 3 Nephi 27:27 where Jesus says, 'Therefore, what manner of men ought ye to be? Verily I say unto you, even as I am.'

I hated and loved my prison experience. Looking back on it, it turned out that I am all the better for it. You can be, as well, if it is what you choose. I think about many of you often and I wish that I could tell you how much you have affected my life, but I ain't coming back. I love and miss you. Through you, I became a better person, but I did most of the work. Through my experience with you, I learned things I never had before, like honesty, integrity, values, feelings, hope, and compassion. It was in prison that I found freedom. It was through living a lifetime of lies that I became a slave. I am a person of honesty and integrity now and I do the best that I can. Again, thank you." (He signed his name and prison number.)

After I first read the things he wrote, we talked a while and he told me some additional things that I think you should hear. He told me that when he first got in prison, he had a very hard time. He was a sexual offender and he was afraid that somebody would kill him in prison. He said that it turned out that he was safe most of the time when he was in prison. I asked him about that and he said, "There are things that happen. Not everybody's safe all the time. I had a couple of close calls." He said that he was much safer than he thought at first. Then he said, "Let me tell you something else. You and all the LDS volunteers are 100% safe when you are in the prison."

I asked, "Why is that?"

He answered, "They would have to go through a lot of men before they could get to you." I've thought about that statement from him a lot and I believe that it's true. I think if the bad guys were coming, you and I would be fighting back to back. You'd be on my side and I'd be on yours. (There were many voices of agreement from the group.) He also told me that he has a very good friend here who gets out next year. He said, "When he gets out, I will be there."

My friend also told me that things were the lowest for him during his first few months in prison. He felt confused, lost, lonely, and afraid. He said one night it was very bad and he was thinking about suicide. He prayed with intense agony, "I just need somebody to talk to." Right after that prayer, these words came into his head: "I am here, and I love you, and I will listen." Yesterday, with tears running down his face, he said, "I know that Jesus walks the halls of the prison."

I had heard those words for the first time a week earlier. On our way out of the prison, Brother Udy and I were talking about several things related to his mission here. Suddenly, Brother Udy looked at me and said, with great feeling, "I know that Jesus walks the halls of this prison." That was a new thought to me. I knew that Jesus walked the halls of the temples but I had never thought about him walking the halls of prisons. In the last two weeks, first Brother Udy, and then my friend, have both told me that they have learned from their own experience that Jesus walks these halls. I believe them.

My friend said that the moment when the Lord said, "I am here, and I love you, and I will listen," was the greatest spiritual experience he's ever had in his life. There were other times when he heard the "still small voice." "One time," he said, "the still small voice said, 'If you do this, you will go to prison.' I didn't listen." Because of the circumstances related to his offense he said, "There were some people who said I was not to blame." And then he looked me right in the eye and said, "But I was."

Maybe some of you have had experiences similar to his. Maybe you have not. I am here to tell you that he was very anxious to share these things with you. He and I both hope that the things he has passed on to you today will help you. I'm not an expert on prison, nor on the things that you have to go through here. If you were to ask me questions about the legalities and the injustices, I would not know the answers. However, I would like to share some more things from the scriptures that I believe will help you. There is a story in the Old Testament that applies to your situation.

There was a great man in the Old Testament named Abraham. Abraham had a son named Isaac. Abraham was known as the friend of God. His son, Isaac, followed in his footsteps. Isaac had a son who was also a great man named Jacob. Jacob's name was changed to Israel. Jacob and Israel are the same person. Jacob had four wives and twelve sons. The twelve tribes of Israel descended from Jacob's sons. Most of the scriptures in the Old Testament are about what happened with the tribes or House of Israel.

One of Jacob's sons was named Joseph. Joseph was one of the youngest sons, but he was the firstborn son of Jacob's wife Rachel. In those days there was a patriarchal government so Jacob was the leader. Generally speaking, the oldest son became the next leader. With four wives, there were four first sons and there were some very strong feelings about who should be the next leader. Some of those sons were not worthy to become the next spiritual leader. Jacob gave his son Joseph a garment that has become known as the "coat of many colors."

Even though Joseph was one of the youngest, Jacob designated him as the next patriarchal leader by giving him that coat. Some of the older brothers were not at all happy about that. Genesis 37:4 says, "And when his brethren saw that their father loved him more than all his brethren, they hated him, and could not speak peaceably unto him." Joseph also had a spiritual gift of having and interpreting dreams. His brothers hated him more because of his dreams and his interpretations of the dreams that showed he was, indeed, to be a leader over them.

Eventually, the brothers were out tending the flocks in a distant place. Jacob sent Joseph out to check on them. As he approached his brothers, they saw him coming,

> And when they saw him afar off, even before he came near unto them, they conspired against him to slay him. And they said one to another, Behold, this dreamer cometh. Come now therefore, and let us slay him, and cast him into some pit, and we will say, Some evil beast hath devoured him: and we shall see what will become of his dreams. (Genesis 37:18-20)

One of the brothers said that they should not kill Joseph, so they threw him in a pit instead. A caravan came by on its way to Egypt. Some of the brothers got him out of the pit, tied him up, gagged him, and sold him as a slave to the caravan. Then some of the brothers took his coat, ripped it up and put goat's blood on it. They took it back to their father, Jacob and lied that a wild beast killed Joseph and the bloody coat was all they could find. Jacob tore his own clothes, went into mourning, and refused to be comforted.

Jacob mourned for many years over his son, Joseph, thinking he was dead. Meanwhile, the caravan of the Midianites went to Egypt and Joseph was sold to a man named Potiphar. One translation says that Potiphar was chief of the Pharaoh's guards, but another one says that he was chief of the slaughterers. At any rate, Joseph was sold to him as a slave and he went to work for Potiphar.

Even as a slave, Joseph prospered.

> And his master [Potiphar], saw that the LORD was with him, and that the LORD made all that he did to prosper in his hand. And Joseph found grace in his sight, and he served him: and he made him overseer over his house, and all that he had he put into his hand. (Genesis 39:3-4)

As near as we can tell, Joseph was seventeen years old when he was sold as a slave. We assume that he was Potiphar's slave for a few years before he was promoted to overseer of Potiphar's house and all that he had. He probably served in that position for several more years. Eventually, Potiphar's wife was attracted to Joseph. The Bible does not tell us her name, but the apocryphal *Book of Jasher* says that her name was Zelica.

> And he [Potiphar] left all that he had in Joseph's hand; and he knew not ought he had, save the bread which he did eat. And Joseph was *a* goodly person, and well favoured. And it came to pass after these things, that his master's wife cast her eyes upon Joseph; and she said, Lie with me. But he refused, and said unto his master's wife, Behold, my master wotteth not what is with me in the house, and he hath committed all that he hath to my hand; There is none greater in this house than I; neither hath he kept back any thing from me but thee, because thou art his wife: how then can I do this great wickedness, and sin against God? And it came to pass, as she spake to Joseph day by day, that he hearkened not unto her, to lie by her, or to be with her. And it came to pass about this time, that Joseph went into the house to do his business; and there was none of the men of the house there within. And she caught him by his

garment, saying, Lie with me: and he left his garment in her hand, and fled, and got him out. And it came to pass, when she saw that he had left his garment in her hand, and was fled forth, That she called unto the men of her house, and spake unto them, saying, See, he hath brought in an Hebrew unto us to mock us; he came in unto me to lie with me, and I cried with a loud voice: And it came to pass, when he heard that I lifted up my voice and cried, that he left his garment with me, and fled, and got him out. And she laid up his garment by her, until his lord came home. And she spake unto him according to these words, saying, The Hebrew servant, which thou hast brought unto us, came in unto me to mock me: And it came to pass, as I lifted up my voice and cried, that he left his garment with me, and fled out. And it came to pass, when his master heard the words of his wife, which she spake unto him, saying, After this manner did thy servant to me; that his wrath was kindled. And Joseph's master took him, and put him into the prison, a place where the king's prisoners were bound: and he was there in the prison. (Genesis 39:6-20)

Joseph was a slave for years and then he was thrown in prison. Why? What did he do to deserve that? He didn't really do anything to his brothers except say things that were irritating to them. At Potiphar's place, he did the best he could to be a good servant and he resisted temptation. He consistently tried to do the right thing and what did it get him? It got him slavery and prison.

There may be a few of you here who are innocent. I've heard that lots of prisoners say that they're innocent, it's not their fault, and they were falsely accused. I assume that's not actually the case with most of you. I assume that most of you are here because you in reality broke the law. But Joseph actually was innocent.

We don't know how long Joseph was a slave and how long he was in prison, but we know that he got out of prison when he was thirty years old and he was about seventeen years old when he went to Egypt. That means that Joseph spent about thirteen years either as a slave or prisoner. If you were Joseph, do you think you might have been feeling discouraged? Do some of you feel that way now? I think that it would be hard to be here without some feelings of frustration and bitterness.

Joseph was in prison for longer than most of you will be, and the prison he was in was a lot worse than this one.

> But the LORD was with Joseph, and shewed him mercy, and gave him favour in the sight of the keeper of the prison. And the keeper of the prison committed to Joseph's hand all the prisoners that were in the prison; and whatsoever they did there, he was the doer of it. The keeper of the prison looked not to any thing that was under his hand; because the LORD was with him, and that which he did, the LORD made it to prosper. (Genesis 39:21-23)

While Joseph was in prison, his attitude and behavior were outstanding. He was so helpful and trustworthy that he was promoted to be the prison overseer. Because of his faithfulness and this promotion, he was able to help and bless the other prisoners.

In Egypt, the king was called Pharaoh. He had two of his personal servants cast into prison because he suspected them of being involved in a plot to kill him. After they were cast into prison, they both had separate but vivid dreams. Since Joseph had a spiritual gift to interpret dreams, he offered to help them. To briefly summarize, Joseph told the chief butler that his dream meant that he would be released from prison and restored to his former position. Joseph asked him to talk with Pharaoh about getting him out of prison. Then Joseph told the chief baker that his dream meant that he would be executed. What Joseph told each man happened within three days.

Two years later, Pharaoh had a dramatic dream which upset him. None of his wise men could give him a satisfactory interpretation. The chief butler remembered that Joseph could interpret dreams and told Pharaoh about him. Pharaoh commanded that Joseph be cleaned up and brought to him. Through the Spirit of the Lord, Joseph was able to interpret Pharaoh's dream and give him wise counsel related to a coming famine. Pharaoh was so impressed that he released Joseph from prison and appointed him to be his advisor and second in command of all Egypt.

Joseph saved many lives in Egypt by preparing the country for the famine. Subsequently, he forgave his brothers and arranged for his whole family to come to Egypt. The rest of the story is great, but today we need to stop there and discuss a few things. What can we learn from Joseph and how does it apply to you? Observe that Joseph managed to turn every experience, even bad ones, into something good.

> This ability to turn everything into something good appears to be a godly characteristic. Our Heavenly Father always seems able to do this. Everything, no matter how dire, becomes a victory to the Lord. Joseph, although a slave and wholly undeserving of this fate, nevertheless remained faithful to the Lord and continued to live the commandments and made something very good of his degrading circumstances. People like this cannot be defeated, because they will not give up. (Hartman Rector Jr., "Live Above the Law to Be Free," *Ensign*, January 1973 .)

One of the greatest things about Joseph was that he could not be kept down. Whatever happened to him, he did not give up. He did not lose faith. He could not be overcome by discouragement. He had it as bad as or worse than you, but no matter what, he continued to try to do the right thing, have faith, and be kind and loving regardless of his circumstances.

Most of you here are descendants of Joseph through his son, Ephraim. Your many, many times great-grandfather, Joseph, spent about thirteen years in prison even though he was innocent. Some of you might be tempted to say, "I don't believe in God anymore because he let bad stuff happen to me. People have been mean to me and I'm going to be mean back." But it does not have to be that way. No matter how bad your circumstances are, try to remember that the Lord loves you. He will help you to be good. Even more than that, he will help you to be the kind of person who helps other people to be good and be happy.

It's your choice. Are you going to follow Joseph's example? Are you going to recognize that Jesus loves the people in prison? Will you return his love and help others to feel it? It's your choice. You have your agency. You decide. But let me tell you something, whatever choice you decide will determine how happy you are here and how happy you'll be when you get out of here.

If you want to be happy here, and if you want to be happy out there, you can do it in spite of horrible circumstances. You can do it the way Joseph did. You may not be able to do it by yourself, but I testify to you that the Lord loves you and he will help you. I have a friend who was here two years ago. We have talked about him today and he has offered you words of advice. He did the best he could while he was here and he is continuing to choose the right now that he is out of here. It is my hope and prayer that all of us, wherever we are, will always remember that the Lord loves us, and that we will follow Joseph's example. I say these things in the name of Jesus Christ. Amen.

Lesson Application

1. How can you experience more of the Lord's love in your life?

2. What do you need to do to follow Joseph's example?

3. Following Christ should include doing something to help prisoners. They need more help while in prison. They need more help finding jobs and housing, and friendship after they get out. Carefully consider what you can safely and wisely do to help prisoners and former prisoners.

4. How can these same principles be applied to those who are in prisons of addiction, emotional prisons, or spiritual prisons?

CHAPTER 35
The Law of Christ

"Whatsoever thou shalt bind on earth shall be bound in heaven."
(Matthew 16:19)

The Law of the Melchizedek Priesthood and the Law of the Levitical/Aaronic Priesthood are different in some important ways. They Law of the Levitical Priesthood is a lesser law, and does not contain all of the powers, rights and ordinances of the Melchizedek Priesthood. From the time of Moses until the time of Christ, most of the Old Testament people lived under the Law of Moses. The Law of Moses was administered by the Levitical/Aaronic Priesthood. When Christ came, he fulfilled the Law of Moses and restored to the earth the "Holy Priesthood after the order of the Son of God." In order to avoid too frequent repetition of the name of deity, this is generally called the Melchizedek Priesthood (D&C 107:3-4). Many of the Old Testament laws were fulfilled (discontinued) by Christ but some of them remained the same. For example, animal sacrifices were discontinued, yet the Ten Commandments were an important part of the new covenant.

The Melchizedek Priesthood was first made known to Adam, and the patriarchs and prophets in every dispensation had this authority. When the children of Israel failed to live up to the privileges and covenants of the

Melchizedek Priesthood, the Lord took away the higher
law and gave them a lesser priesthood and a lesser law.
These were called the Aaronic Priesthood and the Law of
Moses." ("Melchizedek Priesthood", *Bible Dictionary*, 730)

This was verified when John the Baptist compared his
mission and power to the mission and power of Christ. John
said, "I indeed baptize you with water unto repentance: but
he that cometh after me is mightier than I, whose shoes I am
not worthy to bear: he shall baptize you with the Holy Ghost,
and with fire." (Matthew 3:11) John explained that he had the
authority of the Levitical or Aaronic Priesthood, which includes
the authority to baptize with water. Christ brought back the
authority of the Melchizedek Priesthood which included the
baptism of fire.

One of the biggest problems in the New Testament Church
was the conflict between the apostles and the Judaizers
(members of the church who believed that they still needed to
live the Law of Moses). Consequently, the Apostle Paul found
it necessary to repeatedly teach them that they could not be
saved by the Law (of Moses). He also taught that they could
not be saved by the works of the Law (of Moses). Sometimes
the word Torah (meaning the first five books of the Bible) is
actually translated as Law. It is important to remember that
whenever a scripture suggests that you should not follow the
Law, it is not talking about the Law of Christ. Church members
in New Testament times would never have imagined that in
the latter days many would believe that Paul taught that it was
unnecessary to follow the Law of Christ.

A few years ago, a bishop asked me to talk with a member
of his ward who was in the process of leaving the church. This
man argued against the church in the same way that I have heard
hundreds of times. He said that we did not need to have baptism,

the gift of the Holy Ghost, or to keep the Ten Commandments. He said we did not need to obey any of the laws and ordinances of the gospel as it was taught by Christ and Paul in the New Testament. He argued that the only thing that we needed to be saved was to accept Christ as our Savior. He thought that it was actually evil to connect salvation with good works.

The doctrine he propounded was not biblical, even though he said that he had twenty scriptures as proof. He got out his list and we started going through them. One said you cannot be saved by the works of the law. I showed him that in the surrounding verses Paul was talking about the works of the Law of Moses, specifically circumcision. The next scripture said that we are not saved by works lest any man should boast. I explained to him how that one also was talking about the works of the Law of Moses. We went through about ten scriptures that were saying basically the same thing and each time I showed him that it was talking about the Law of Moses. I asked if we really needed to go over the same thing again and again since none of those scriptures meant what he thought they did. Finally, he said, "Well, I guess I don't understand about the Law of Moses." His whole concept of salvation was based on scriptures that he clearly did not understand. I suggested that before he left the church it would be a good idea for him to learn enough about the Bible to tell the difference between when the scriptures are talking about the Law of Moses or the Law of Christ.

Of course, this man is not alone in his misunderstanding. There are many wonderful Christians out there whose whole concept of salvation is based on a misinterpretation of what Paul said about the Law. You probably have heard such arguments before, sometimes even coming from members of our church. A Sunday School student once said, "Some of the best missionary work I've done has been to help straighten out people who have been members of the Church longer than I have, who don't understand this issue." Here's the thing: We really believe in having faith in Christ. We know that we have to be saved by his grace. What we don't believe in is using Christ's name to teach that you don't have to keep his commandments.

Eternal Marriages and Families

Another common, and closely related misunderstanding of the scriptures comes from Matthew 22:23-28 which says,

> The same day came to him the Sadducees, which say that there is no resurrection, and asked him, Saying, Master, Moses said, If a man die, having no children, his brother shall marry his wife, and raise up seed unto his brother. Now there were with us seven brethren: and the first, when he had married a wife, deceased, and, having no issue, left his wife unto his brother: Likewise the second also, and the third, unto the seventh. And last of all the woman died also. Therefore in the resurrection whose wife shall she be of the seven? for they all had her?

Those who misunderstand the scriptures use this verse to argue that there is no marriage in the resurrection and no marriage in heaven. Therefore, we should not expect to have eternal marriages and families. We should just plan on living a heavenly, separate, single life forever. I suggest that before you give up on your eternal family that we review the easy answer to this biblically ignorant argument.

Consider the context of this question and answer. The question was asked by the Sadducees, who did not believe in the resurrection. Therefore, it is a trap or trick question with the intent of making Jesus look foolish, while promoting their doctrine. The Sadducees were trying to make the point that there can't be a resurrection because this woman can't be with seven different husbands in the resurrection. Continuing in

Matthew 22:29, "Jesus answered and said unto them, Ye do err, not knowing the scriptures, nor the power of God. For in the resurrection they neither marry, nor are given in marriage, but are as the angels of God in heaven." The way this verse reads tends to add to the confusion. However, Jesus was referring to a specific custom of the time: Levirate marriage. Levirate marriage is

> The custom of a widow marrying her deceased husband's brother or sometimes a near heir. The word has nothing to do with the name Levi or the biblical Levites, but is so called because of the Latin *levir*, meaning "husband's brother," connected with the English suffix -*ate*, thus constituting levirate. This system of marriage is designated in Deuteronomy 25:5-10. ("Levirate Marriage," *Bible Dictionary*, 724)

Under which law did the marriages that the Sadducees asked about take place? The answer is obvious. Their question actually included the phrase "Master, Moses said…" It could only have been The Law of Moses since that is the only law they had at that time. The woman was married to all seven men according to the Levirate marriage provision of the Law of Moses. Next question, "Does the Levitical/Aaronic priesthood have the power to seal people together in eternal marriage?" Of course, the answer is no. Therefore, if Jesus was going to give a full answer, he would have said something like, "You do not understand the priesthood. Levirate marriage is not binding in heaven." Had this not been an adversarial question coming from a group of people who did not even believe in the resurrection, he might have said much more. He might have gone on to explain about the Melchizedek Priesthood and the sealing powers which had been restored to Peter (Matthew 16:19) so that families could be sealed together forever. But of course, he did not, because discussing such things with that hostile audience would have been "casting pearls before swine."

In another time and place, Jesus did explain these things to a more receptive audience saying,

> I am the Lord thy God; and give you this commandment—that no man shall come unto the Father but by me or by my word, which is my law saith the Lord. And everything that is in the world, whether it be ordained of men, by thrones, or principalities, or powers, or things of name, whatsoever they may be, that are not by me or by my word, saith the Lord, shall be thrown down, and shall not remain after men are dead, neither in nor after the resurrection, saith the Lord your God. For whatsoever things remain are by me; and whatsoever things are not by me shall be shaken and destroyed. Therefore, if a man marry him a wife in the world, and he marry her not by me nor by my word, and he covenant with her so long as he is in the world and she with him, their covenant and marriage are not of force when they are dead, and when they are out of the world; therefore, they are not bound by any law when they are out of the world. Therefore, when they are out of the world they neither marry nor are given in marriage; but are appointed angels in heaven, which angels are ministering servants, to minister for those who are worthy of a far more, and an exceeding, and an eternal weight of glory. (D&C 132:12-16)

Notice that Jesus used some of the exact same words as found in Matthew 22. He did that so there would be no misunderstanding.

Peter held the sealing keys. Jesus said,

> And I say unto thee, That thou art Peter, and upon this rock I will build my church; and the gates of hell shall not prevail against it. And I will give unto thee the keys of the kingdom of heaven: and whatsoever thou shalt bind on earth shall be bound in heaven: and whatsoever thou

shalt loose on earth shall be loosed in heaven. (Matthew 16:18, 19)

In the Doctrine and Covenants, Jesus explained,

> And again, verily I say unto you, if a man marry a wife by my word, which is my law, and by the new and everlasting covenant, and it is sealed unto them by the Holy Spirit of Promise, by him who is anointed, unto whom I have appointed this power and the keys of this priesthood…it shall be done unto them in all things whatsoever my servant hath put upon them, in time, and through all eternity; and shall be of full force when they are out of the world; and they shall pass by the angels, and the gods, which are set there, to their exaltation and glory in all things, as hath been sealed upon their heads, which glory shall be a fulness and a continuation of the seeds forever and ever. (D&C 132:19)

How blessed we are to have the fullness of the gospel with its vision of the eternal nature of marriages and families.

> The ultimate purpose of all we teach is to unite parents and children in faith in the Lord, Jesus Christ, that they are happy at home and sealed in an eternal marriage and linked to their generations and assured of exaltation in the presence of their Heavenly Father. (Boyd K. Packer, "The Shield of Faith." *Ensign,* May 1995)

Ponder this in connection with the following verse:

> In the celestial glory there are three heavens or degrees; And in order to obtain the highest, a man must enter into this order of the priesthood [meaning the new and everlasting covenant of marriage]; And if he does not, he cannot obtain it. He may enter into the other, but that is the end of his kingdom; he cannot have an increase. (Doctrine and Covenants 131:1-4)

These two quotes express some of the fundamental doctrines of our church.

Plural Marriage

Doctrine and Covenants 132 also talks about plural marriage. Plural marriage tends to be a very uncomfortable topic, and some people really struggle with it. They are upset that Joseph Smith, Brigham Young, or anybody else was ever involved in plural marriage. They think it was a big mistake, or worse, terrible and wrong. On the other hand, there are some people who think it is a great idea and want to start living it right now. There are many people in splinter groups who practice plural marriage and are looking for recruits. As soon as you start talking about plural marriage, some people either want to run away or want to run off and live it.

Concerning current plural marriage practices, President Gordon B. Hinckley said,

> I wish to state categorically that this church has nothing whatever to do with those practicing polygamy. They are not members of this church. Most of them have never been members. If any of our members are found to be practicing plural marriage, they are excommunicated; the most serious penalty the church can impose. Not only are those so involved in direct violation of the civil law, they are in violation of the law of this church. (Gordon B. Hinckley, "What are People Asking about Us?", *Ensign*, November 1998)

The law of this church that President Hinckley is referring to came about as a result of the Manifesto, which was issued in 1890.

One of the problems related to the history of plural marriage in the church is an abundance of anti-Mormon propaganda that says Joseph Smith and Brigham Young were horrible men because they participated in plural marriage. Countless books and articles promote that misconception. You should avoid reading those books because they include dishonesty, errors, many false details, and limited truth. You should also avoid most books written by church members on this same topic because they contain a lot of erroneous supposition. If you are really interested in this subject, I recommend reading *Joseph Smith and the Restoration* by Ivan J. Barret, which is out of print but can be purchased as used book. If you have the spiritual and scholastic background to deal with complicated and challenging historical issues, I recommend reading *Joseph Smith's Polygamy*, Volumes 1, 2, and 3, by Brian C. Hales. All three volumes in hardcover total about 1256 pages, at a current cost of about $100. Any study on this topic would seem to be severely lacking if it did not include these books.

In the Book of Mormon, Jacob says that marriage should only include one man and one woman *unless*, "For if I will, saith the Lord of Hosts, raise up seed unto me, I will command my people; otherwise they shall hearken unto these things." (Jacob 2:27, 30) In other words, marriage is supposed to be monogamous unless the Lord specifically commands otherwise. Sometimes, he needs something accomplished, and in order to fulfill his purposes, it is necessary to increase the number of children.

Abraham, Isaac, and Jacob were commanded to have plural marriages. If Jacob had only been married to Rachel there would only have been two tribes of Israel, which would not have included enough people to accomplish the Lord's purposes. There would not have been enough of them to survive and inherit the Promised Land. By the way, having plural husbands instead of plural wives would not increase the number of children very much. The world assumes that the issue is male dominance and sexual desire. They are wrong. The Lord's polygamy is about families, children, and descendants.

In Matthew 8:11 Jesus said that people from all over the world would come into heaven and sit down with Abraham, Isaac, and Jacob. Thus, Christ verified that some of those in heaven practiced plural marriage. Additionally, Jesus also said, "Abraham ... hath entered into his exaltation and sitteth upon his throne." (D&C 132:29)

> In this dispensation, the Lord commanded some of the early saints to practice plural marriage. The prophet Joseph Smith and those closest to him, including Brigham Young and Heber C. Kimball were challenged by this commandment but they obeyed it and church leaders regulated the practice and those entering into it had to be authorized to do so and the marriages had to be performed by the sealing power of the Holy Priesthood. ("Sealed ... for Time and for All Eternity," *Gospel Doctrine Teacher's Manual: Doctrine and Covenants and Church History*, Lesson 31)

Some members of the church have become so upset about the fact that Joseph Smith and other early church leaders lived plural marriage, that they have decided not to believe in the Church anymore. They have decided to walk away from their own eternal marriage covenants. How much sense does it make to give up your eternal family because of something you do not understand and are not required to live?

The Angel Moroni told Joseph that his name would be had for good and evil among all nations, kindreds, tongues and peoples. (Joseph Smith History 1:33) That prophecy has certainly been fulfilled. However, before you start believing that Joseph or Brigham were evil because they participated in plural marriage, consider a few questions. How many of us are descendants of plural marriage? How many were taught the gospel, or have ancestors who were taught by missionaries who were descendants of plural marriage? I have asked these questions in many, many classes. Usually, more than half the students raised their hands in response.

Did you know that most of the church's missionaries, up until the 1980's, were descendants of plural marriage? If we had not had plural marriage in this church, how large would the church's membership be now? The Lord needed to get the Church built up as fast as possible in the latter days in order to be prepared for the Second Coming of Christ. How much different would the world be if the church was less than half the size it is now? How much different would things be for you personally? I would not be a member of the church. I would not have an eternal family. My wife would not be here. My children would not be here.

It's time to quit worrying about whether Joseph or Brigham or your great, great grandpa should have married this wife or that wife. It's time to make sure that you are keeping your covenants and keeping your eternal family together.

In conclusion, I hope you will never be bothered by things related to the differences between the Law of Moses and the Law of Christ. I hope that you will not be bothered by historical people who lived plural marriage when they were commanded to do so. I hope that you are not anxious to live plural marriage. Most of all, I hope all of us will eventually receive every blessing of exaltation connected with the sealing power that was restored to the earth through the prophet Joseph Smith.

Discussion Questions

1. What is your understanding of the differences between the Levitical/Aaronic Priesthood and the Melchizedek Priesthood?
2. How would you respond to someone who told you that you only needed faith to be saved?

3. How can you avoid jeopardizing your eternal family over things that you do not fully understand?

CHAPTER 36
Two Anointings
Anointing by the Sinful Woman

The first anointing of Christ in the New Testament is recorded in the book of Luke. Let's carefully read the account and then review and discuss it.

> And one of the Pharisees desired him that he would eat with him. And he went into the Pharisee's house, and sat down to meat. And, behold, a woman in the city, which was a sinner, when she knew that Jesus sat at meat in the Pharisee's house, brought an alabaster box of ointment, And stood at his feet behind him weeping, and began to wash his feet with tears, and did wipe them with the hairs of her head, and kissed his feet, and anointed them with the ointment. Now when the Pharisee which had bidden him saw it, he spake within himself, saying, This man, if he were a prophet, would have known who and what manner of woman this is that toucheth him: for she is a sinner. And Jesus answering said unto him, Simon, I have somewhat to say unto thee. And he saith, Master, say on. There was a certain creditor which had two debtors: the one owed five hundred pence, and the other fifty. And when they had nothing to pay, he frankly forgave them both. Tell me therefore, which of them will love him most? Simon answered and said, I suppose that he, to whom he forgave most. And he said unto him, Thou hast rightly judged. And

he turned to the woman, and said unto Simon, Seest thou this woman? I entered into thine house, thou gavest me no water for my feet: but she hath washed my feet with tears, and wiped them with the hairs of her head. Thou gavest me no kiss: but this woman since the time I came in hath not ceased to kiss my feet. My head with oil thou didst not anoint: but this woman hath anointed my feet with ointment. Wherefore I say unto thee, Her sins, which are many, are forgiven; for she loved much: but to whom little is forgiven, the same loveth little. And he said unto her, Thy sins are forgiven. And they that sat at meat with him began to say within themselves, Who is this that forgiveth sins also? And he said to the woman, Thy faith hath saved thee; go in peace. (Luke 7:36-50)

In his books *Doctrinal New Testament Commentary* and *The Mortal Messiah*, Bruce R. McConkie emphatically affirms that this woman was, "Not Mary Magdalene and not Mary of Bethany, both of whom were righteous women of good character." (DNTC, 1:264-265; MM, 2:207, Note 4)

Let's refer back to Luke 7:36: "And one of the Pharisees desired him that he would eat with him and he went to the Pharisee's house and sat down to meat." That's very significant. Up to this point in Christ's ministry, the Pharisees have been his enemies. They have not been interested in what he has to say. They're only interested in opposing him and killing him. This is the only time in the New Testament when Jesus was invited to eat at a Pharisee's house. If Simon was sincere, this could have been a great breakthrough.

James E. Talmage wrote,

It was a custom of the times to treat a distinguished guest with marked attention, to receive him with a kiss of welcome, to provide water to wash the dust from his feet, and oil for the anointing of the hair of the head and the beard. All these courteous attentions were omitted by Simon. (*Jesus the Christ*, 261)

Simon had not treated Jesus as an honored guest. In short, Simon treated him insolently.

"Jesus took his place, probably on one of the divans or couches on which it was usual to partly sit, partly recline, while eating. Such an attitude would place the feet of the person outward from the table." (*Jesus the Christ*, 261) They leaned on their left arms and ate with their right hands, because the right hand was considered to be the clean hand.

Verse 37 introduces another visitor to Simon's house, "And behold, a woman in the city, which was a sinner." What kind of sins would she have committed that she would be commonly known as a sinner? One possibility is that she was a thief. Another possibility is adultery. Because of her status, she would not be welcome at the synagogue or at a Pharisee's house. By entering his house she might have been exposing herself to a flogging. But she went anyway. "When she knew that Jesus sat at meat in the Pharisee's house, brought an alabaster box of ointment." (Luke 7:37) Most anointings in those days were done with olive oil. This anointing was done with expensive ointment.

She "stood at his feet behind him weeping and began to wash his feet with tears and did wipe them with the hairs of her head and kissed his feet and anointed them with the ointment." (Luke 7:38)

The woman washed his feet with her tears and dried them with her hair. Then she rubbed ointment on his feet. If a woman you didn't know was doing that with your feet, brethren, how would you feel about it? Sisters, if a woman you didn't know was doing that with your husband's feet, how would you feel?

Our culture is different than theirs but this is still something more intimate than would be expected between strangers.

"Now when the Pharisee which had bidden him saw it, he spake within himself, saying, This man, if he were a prophet, would have known who and what manner of woman this is that toucheth him: for she is a sinner." (Luke 7:39) You see, Simon has latched on to something that he thinks proves Jesus is not a prophet or holy man. Note here that Simon is very judgmental of the woman, and of Jesus.

Jesus answers what Simon is thinking by saying, "Simon, I have somewhat to say unto thee. And he saith, Master, say on. There was a certain creditor which had two debtors: the one owed five hundred pence, and the other fifty. And when they had nothing to pay, he frankly forgave them both. Tell me therefore, which of them will love him most?" (Luke 7:40-42)

Notice that Jesus easily established himself as the master who was asking the student a question which requires a response. The roles have been reversed. Simon started out thinking that he was the master and Jesus was a fraud. In just a few words, Jesus has completely turned the tables. Simon did not want to look stupid so he tried to give the best answer he could. "Simon answered and said, I suppose that he to whom he forgave the most." And Jesus says, "Thou hast judged rightly." (Luke 7:43)

Let's review the circumstances. Jesus was the guest of a man who was in a position of power, influence, and wealth. The woman was not considered significant or worthy to even be in Simon's house. If you were in Jesus' position you might be tempted to appease the man at the expense of the woman, but that is not what he did. Jesus looked at the woman and spoke to Simon saying,

Simon, Seest thou this woman? I entered into thine house, thou gavest me no water for my feet: but she hath washed my feet with tears, and wiped them with the hairs of her head. Thou gavest me no kiss: but this woman since the time I came in hath not ceased to kiss my feet. My head with oil thou didst not anoint: but this woman hath anointed my feet with ointment. Wherefore I say unto thee, Her sins, which are many, are forgiven; for she loved much: but to whom little is forgiven, the same loveth little. (Luke 7:44-47)

In other words, "Simon, the woman you consider to be unworthy loves much and is forgiven, and you are rude, judgmental, and remain unforgiven." Jesus concludes the discussion by saying to the woman, "Thy faith hath saved thee; go in peace." (Luke 7:50)

I would like to ask you to imagine yourself in the roles of Jesus, Simon the Pharisee, and the woman. When doing so, what do you think? How do you feel? Symbolically speaking, every one of us has been in the place of Simon the Pharisee. Every one of us has sometimes been too judgmental when we should have been loving and forgiving. Each one of us should ask ourselves, "Do I really want to be like Simon the Pharisee?"

Every one of us in one way or another has also been in the place of the woman. We have all committed sins and need forgiveness. It takes courage and faith to confront sin in your own life and to talk with the bishop. All of us can learn from the example of this woman. If she could have that kind of faith and courage, we can too.

The most important thing we need to do is come to Christ. We have to rely on the Atonement. We need to come to him humbly, on bended knee, setting our pride aside, asking for forgiveness. When we feel and ask it deeply enough, there will be tears. Sometimes there's not enough depth of feeling in our repentance because we take it too lightly.

When I asked the students of one class to imagine themselves in Jesus' place, feeling what he felt, Brooke answered, "I think that he felt grateful. I think he felt compassion for her."

I am sure Jesus felt gratitude, compassion, and love. When you approach the Lord, or the bishop, with faith and courage, trying to repent, the response will be gratitude, compassion, love, and forgiveness.

But what about the Pharisee? Jesus loves the Pharisee too. He gave the Pharisee exactly what he needed at that time. We don't know how the Pharisee responded to what Jesus said. If I was in Simon's place, I would have felt humbled. I hope I would have said, "Oh my goodness! I'm on the wrong track," and turned around in a big hurry. Most of the Pharisees did not change, but a few did.

Reading and understanding this account has made a difference in my life. It has changed the way I feel about the Lord and has made a difference in the way I feel about and treat other people. I hope and pray that it will make a difference in you.

Anointing by Mary of Bethany

Now let's read and discuss another anointing recorded by John, Matthew, and Mark.

> Then Jesus six days before the passover came to Bethany, where Lazarus was which had been dead, whom he raised from the dead. There they made him a supper; and Martha served: but Lazarus was one of them that sat at the table with him. Then took Mary a pound of ointment of spikenard, very costly, and anointed the feet of Jesus, and wiped his feet with her hair: and the house was filled with the odour of the ointment. Then saith one of his disciples, Judas Iscariot, Simon's son, which should betray him, Why

was not this ointment sold for three hundred pence, and given to the poor? This he said, not that he cared for the poor; but because he was a thief, and had the bag, and bare what was put therein. Then said Jesus, Let her alone: against the day of my burying hath she kept this. For the poor always ye have with you; but me ye have not always. (John 12:2-8)

Now when Jesus was in Bethany, in the house of Simon the leper, There came unto him a woman having an alabaster box of very precious ointment, and poured it on his head, as he sat at meat. But when his disciples saw it, they had indignation, saying, To what purpose is this waste? For this ointment might have been sold for much, and given to the poor. When Jesus understood it, he said unto them, Why trouble ye the woman? for she hath wrought a good work upon me. For ye have the poor always with you; but me ye have not always. For in that she hath poured this ointment on my body, she did it for my burial. Verily I say unto you, Wheresoever this gospel shall be preached in the whole world, there shall also this, that this woman hath done, be told for a memorial of her. Then one of the twelve, called Judas Iscariot, went unto the chief priests, And said unto them, What will ye give me, and I will deliver him unto you? And they covenanted with him for thirty pieces of silver. And from that time he sought opportunity to betray him. (Matthew 26:6-16)

And being in Bethany in the house of Simon the leper, as he sat at meat, there came a woman having an alabaster box of ointment of spikenard very precious; and she brake the box, and poured it on his head. And there were some that had indignation within themselves, and said, Why was this waste of the ointment made? For it might have been sold for more than three hundred pence, and have been given to the poor. And they murmured against her. And Jesus said, Let her alone; why trouble ye her? she hath wrought a good work on me. For ye have the poor with you always, and whensoever ye will ye may do them good:

but me ye have not always. She hath done what she could: she is come aforehand to anoint my body to the burying. Verily I say unto you, Wheresoever this gospel shall be preached throughout the whole world, this also that she hath done shall be spoken of for a memorial of her. And Judas Iscariot, one of the twelve, went unto the chief priests, to betray him unto them. (Mark 14:3-10)

These three accounts have some differences, but there are at least six common elements. It is approximately the same time and the same place. Most of the same people seem to be there. Each account describes an anointing. The same objection to the anointing is brought up in each account. Each time the objector is rebuked by Jesus in the same way. The possibility that these three accounts describe more than one event is extremely remote. However, it is obvious that this is a different anointing than the one described by Luke in Galilee more than a year previous.

In his book *The Mortal Messiah* Bruce R. McConkie refers to the Bethany anointing as a sacred ordinance. (MM, 3;333-337) Heber C. Kimball received a similar anointing under the direction of Joseph Smith and Brigham Young, which helps verify that both Jesus' head and feet were anointed even though both are not mentioned in all three gospel accounts. (Kimball, *On the Potter's Wheel*, 55-57)

It appears that this anointing is related to the doctrine of becoming kings and queens and priests and priestesses. It also seems to be part of an ordinance associated with temple sealings and having one's calling and election made sure .

Lesson Insight

Note that the Bethany anointing is what pushed Judas over the edge. The very next thing reported is that Judas, "Went unto the chief priests, And said unto them, What will ye give me, and I will deliver him unto you … And from that time he sought opportunity to betray him. (Matthew 26:14-16) Judas did not understand or have reverence for a sacred ordinance and tried to belittle it by saying that it would have been better to give to the poor. Not only that, but his motive was tainted because, "This he said, not that he cared for the poor; but because he was a thief, and had the bag, and bare what was put therein." (John 12:6)

First Judas failed to comprehend, then he sought to belittle, then he began to betray. Judas is not the only one to follow this tragic course. In fact, a great many people have said something like this, "It is a waste of money for the Church to build and maintain beautiful temples. The Church should use that money to help the poor." After thus belittling the temple and ordinances, which they do not comprehend, they often proceed to oppose or betray the Savior and those who are devoted to him. At the same time they hypocritically ignore the fact the Church does more for the poor than they do.

We must be careful to avoid making the same mistakes Judas did: ignorance, desecration, betrayal. We must also be careful to avoid the mistakes of Simon the Pharisee: pride, lack of love, failure to repent.

Discussion Questions

1. How are you going to avoid being like Simon the Pharisee?
2. What have you learned from the sinful woman?
3. What did you learn from putting yourself in the place of Jesus?
4. What do you think about Jesus siding with Mary, against Judas?
5. What did the last part of this chapter help teach you about sacred ordinances?

CHAPTER 37

We Are Not Forsaken

"And behold, Enoch saw the day of the coming of the Son of Man, even in the flesh; and his soul rejoiced, saying: The Righteous is lifted up, and the Lamb is slain from the foundation of the world; and through faith I am in the bosom of the Father, and behold, Zion is with me." (Moses 4:47)

Messiah or Priestcraft

After Jesus submitted to arrest on the Mount of Olives, "Then the band and the captain and officers of the Jews took Jesus, and bound him, And led him away to Annas first; for he was father in law to Caiaphas, which was the high priest that same year." (John 18:13)

The Chief Priest and his cohorts were thoroughly wicked and corrupt.

> During this era the Chief Priest (who controlled the temple) was appointed by the Romans, with the selection being influenced by bribery... [Jesus] knew that the chief priests were evil enough to kill anyone who threatened their power, income, or status." (GVS, *Concise Harmony of the Four Gospels*, page 23, note 22)

Annas was similar to the Godfather of a modern-day crime family. He and his group pretended to be righteous, but they were using priestcraft to acquire power and wealth. Jesus started and ended his mortal ministry by casting part of their organization out of the temple, saying, "Ye have made it a den of thieves." (Matthew 21:13; see also John 2:14-17)

Annas, Caiaphas, and the rest of their crime family used deceit and fraud to swindle and control the faithful. They perceived Jesus to be a threat and tried to trap or kill him for most of his ministry. Concerning those who practice such priestcraft, Jesus said, "Even so ye also outwardly appear righteous unto men, but within ye are full of hypocrisy and iniquity... Ye serpents, ye generation of vipers, how can ye escape the damnation of hell?" (Matthew 23:28, 33)

The following three quotations from *The Book of Mormon* contain significant information about priestcraft:

"He commandeth that there shall be no priestcrafts; for, behold, priestcrafts are that men preach and set themselves up for a light unto the world, that they may get gain and praise of the world; but they seek not the welfare of Zion." (2 Nephi 26:29)

> But Alma said unto him: Behold, this is the first time that priestcraft has been introduced among this people. And behold, thou art not only guilty of priestcraft, but hast endeavored to enforce it by the sword; and were priestcraft to be enforced among this people it would prove their entire destruction. (Alma 1:12)

The following quotation identifies priestcraft as a primary factor in bringing about the crucifixion of Christ, and the subsequent devastation and scattering of the tribe of Judah.

> But because of priestcrafts and iniquities, they at Jerusalem will stiffen their necks against him, that he be crucified. Wherefore, because of their iniquities, destructions, famines, pestilences, and bloodshed shall come

upon them; and they who shall not be destroyed shall be scattered among all nations. (2 Nephi 10:5-6)

Behold Your King

The chief priests eventually used a mock trial to condemn Jesus to death. Under Roman rule they were not allowed to execute people, so they delivered Jesus to Pilate, the Roman governor, demanding that he carry out the death sentence. Pilate, "Knew that for envy they had delivered him" (Matthew 27:18) and didn't want to have Jesus executed. Pilate's wife "Sent unto him, saying, Have thou nothing to do with that just man: for I have suffered many things this day in a dream because of him." (Matthew 27:19)

Pilate tried to appease the people and let Jesus go. "Now at that feast the governor was wont to release unto the people a prisoner, whom they would" (Matthew 27:15-16). Tradition deemed that a prisoner be set free during the time of the feast. At the time Jesus was brought to Pilate, the prison held a notable prisoner, called Barabbas. It appears that Barabbas was the leader of a band of robbers and murderers similar to the Gadiaton robbers in the Book of Mormon. Pilate must have believed the Jews would rather release Jesus and keep a known villain behind bars.

But the presentation of the choice between Jesus and Barabbas happened early in the morning. Due to the early hour, it is probable that most of the people in attendance were recruited by the chief priests. Therefore,

> The chief priests and elders persuaded the multitude that they should ask [choose] Barabbas, and destroy Jesus. The governor answered and said unto them, Whether of the twain will ye that I release unto you? They said, Barabbas. Pilate saith unto them, What shall I do then with Jesus

which is called Christ? They all say unto him, Let him be crucified. And the governor said, Why, what evil hath he done? But they cried out the more, saying, Let him be crucified. (Matthew 27:20-23)

When Pilate saw that he could prevail nothing, but that rather a tumult was made, he took water, and washed his hands before the multitude, saying, I am innocent of the blood of this just person: see ye to it. Then answered all the people, and said, His blood be on us, and on our children. Then released he Barabbas unto them: and when he had scourged Jesus, he delivered him to be crucified. (Matthew 27:24-26)

John's account of this event gives the following additional information.

Pilate sought to release him: but the Jews cried out, saying, If thou let this man go, thou art not Caesar's friend: whosoever maketh himself a king speaketh against Caesar. When Pilate therefore heard that saying he brought Jesus forth…and saith unto the Jews, Behold your King! But they cried out, Away with him, away with him, Crucify him. Pilate saith unto them, Shall I crucify your King: the chief priests answered, We have no king but Caesar." (John 19:12-15)

The chief priests sought to manipulate Pilate's actions by threatening to frame him as an opponent to Caesar. This tactic apparently worked. Pilate remains accountable for his actions in the case of Jesus' crucifixion, but the chief priests were the primary perpetrators of Jesus' death.

The Day of Atonement

The circumstances just described are related to an interesting practice enacted on the Day of Atonement as set forth in Leviticus chapter 16. The Day of Atonement was held after the Feast of Trumpets and a few days before the Feast of the Tabernacles. Starting in Leviticus 16:7 it says,

> And he shall take the two goats, and present them before the LORD at the door of the tabernacle of the congregation… But the goat, on which the lot fell to be the scapegoat, shall be presented alive before the LORD… Then shall he kill the goat of the sin offering, that is for the people, and bring his blood within the veil… And he shall make an Atonement for the holy place, because of the uncleanness of the children of Israel, and because of their transgressions in all their sins… (Leviticus 16:7-10, 15-16)

> And when he hath made an end of reconciling the holy place, and the tabernacle of the congregation, and the altar, he shall bring the live goat: And Aaron shall lay both his hands upon the head of the live goat, and confess over him all the iniquities of the children of Israel, and all their transgressions in all their sins, putting them upon the head of the goat, and shall send him away by the hand of a fit man into the wilderness: And the goat shall bear upon him all their iniquities unto a land not inhabited: and he shall let go the goat in the wilderness. (Leviticus 16:20-22)

This Old Testament Day of Atonement ritual symbolically represented what was going to happen with Christ in the New Testament. There were two goats. One of them was sacrificed, which was a prophetic representation of Christ and his Atonement. The other goat released into the wilderness symbolically covered with blood and sin was a prophetic representation fulfilled by Barabbas.

In order to tie this all together, let's go back to Matthew 27:25 where the chief priests and others were so blinded by priestcraft that they demanded the crucifixion of Christ, saying, "His blood be on us, and on our children." Think about that. Figuratively, they were saying "Let the responsibility for the death of the Son of God come upon us and our posterity. Let all of our sin and iniquity remain on our heads. Let our fate be connected with that of the scapegoat which was chased into the wilderness."

Let's put this in historical perspective. Most scholars think that Christ was crucified between 30 and 33 A.D. In 70 A.D. (within one generation) Jerusalem was destroyed. It is estimated that about 1.5 million Jews were slain in Jerusalem and the surrounding area. (GVS, *Concise Harmony of the Four Gospels*, page 49, note 175). Those who survived were chased into the world and remained without a country until the nation of Israel was founded in 1948. The responsibility for the death of the Son of God was literally answered upon the heads of those who perpetrated it and upon their posterity for centuries afterward.

Now let's add this all up. The chief priests, who were heavily involved in priestcraft, persuaded the people to choose the robber instead of Jesus, and proclaimed, "We have no king but Caesar." At least thirty five years later the three main things that brought about the destruction and scattering of the tribe of Judah were priestcraft, robbers, and Roman armies." (GVS, *Concise Harmony of the Four Gospels*, page 52, note 216) The Jews rejected Christ and got precisely the three things they chose instead.

However, those who accepted Christ experienced a very different fate. Concerning the destruction of Jerusalem in 70 A.D., James C. Talmage recounted the miraculous escape of those who did heed and follow Christ:

> The warning to all to flee from Jerusalem and Judea to the mountains [Matthew 24:21-37] when the armies would begin to surround the city was so generally heeded by members of the Church, that according to the early Church writers not one Christian perished in the awful siege (see Eusebius, Eccles. Hist., book iii, ch. 5). (James E. Talmage, *Jesus the Christ*, 588, chapter 32, endnote 1.)

History has borne out the promise that following Christ can bring safety and salvation; rejecting him can result in death and destruction.

If you choose to reject Christ, what will you choose, and what will the result be? Will it be something that will give you peace and happiness in the long run? Whoever or whatever we pick instead of Christ isn't going to save us and it isn't going to make us happy. It is shocking to see both the immediate and the long lasting consequences that came to those who rejected Christ in former times, as cited above. We need to make sure we don't make the same mistakes that they did.

On The Cross

Let's move forward now with the scriptural narrative at the time of the crucifixion and discuss some of the words Christ spoke from the cross.

> And when they were come unto a place called Golgotha, that is to say, a place of a skull…they crucified him, and parted his garments, casting lots: that it might be fulfilled which was spoken by the prophet, They parted my garments among them, and upon my vesture did they cast lots. And sitting down they watched him there; And set up over his head his accusation written, THIS IS JESUS THE KING OF THE JEWS. Then were there two thieves crucified with him, one on the right hand, and another on the left. And they that passed by reviled him, wagging their heads And saying… If thou be the Son of God, come down from the cross. Likewise also the chief priests mocking him, with the scribes and elders, said, He saved others; himself he cannot save. If he be the King of Israel, let him now come down from the cross, and we will believe him. He trusted in God; let him deliver him now, if he will have him: for he said, I am the Son of God. (Matthew 27:33-43)

After he had been on the cross for six hours, "Jesus cried with a loud voice, saying, Eli, Eli, lama sabachthani? that is to say, My God, my God, why hast thou forsaken me?" Matthew 27:46; see also Mark 15:25-34)

For many years verse 46 bothered me because Jesus previously told his disciples that he was going to be sacrificed. He had prophesied about it again and again, so it should not have been a surprise to him that he was suffering death on the cross for the sins of mankind, and he should not have felt abandoned in that moment. One thing that has been mentioned in several books and sermons is that maybe the Spirit of God withdrew from Jesus for a while in order to allow him to complete the suffering and the Atonement alone. Another insight is found in Psalm 22, which is referred to by Matthew 27:46, footnote 46a.

Psalms 22:1 says, "My God, my God, why hast thou forsaken me?" That is not a coincidence. At that time, the Bible was not divided into chapters and verses. Therefore, if someone wanted to call attention to a certain psalm, they sometimes recited the first line of that psalm. So, when Jesus said, "My God, my God, why hast thou forsaken me," he was calling attention to what we now know as Psalm 22.

Why would he do that? Let's take a close look at Psalms 22:7-8, "All they that see me laugh me to scorn: they shoot out the lip, they shake the head, saying He trusted on the LORD that he would deliver him: let him deliver him, seeing he delighted in him." Remember Matthew 27:39, "And they that passed by reviled him, wagging their heads..." Note how all this matches exactly.

The real shocker comes in Psalms 22:16, 18: "For dogs have compassed me: the assembly of the wicked have inclosed me: they pierced my hands and my feet ...

They part my garments among them, and cast lots upon my vesture."

So when Jesus quoted Psalm 22 from the cross, in essence he was saying, "When David was prophesying centuries ago about what would happen to the Messiah, he detailed what is happening to me right now, including what you just said to me, and the way you wagged your head while saying it." When Jesus referenced Psalms 22 from the cross he was proving his identity, verifying his mission, and fulfilling ancient prophecy.

This is validated in an excellent Ensign article. "Though the Savior quoted only the first verse, the remainder of the psalm stands as another testimony that He is the promised Messiah, that His suffering fulfilled prophecy, and that he trusted in His Father completely." (Adam C. Olsen, "Never Forsaken," *Ensign*, January 2011.)

The Veil of the Temple

In Matthew 27:51, we learn that right after Christ died on the cross, "The veil of the temple was rent in twain from the top to the bottom; and the earth did quake, and the rocks rent;" Inside the temple was a room called the Holy Place. At the east end of the Holy Place was a veil. On the other side of the veil was the Most Holy Place which is sometimes called the Holy of Holies. Originally, the Ark of the Covenant, representing the presence of God, was kept in the Most Holy Place. When one passed through the veil, symbolically speaking, he entered into the presence of God. So when the veil of the temple ripped open at the death of Christ, the door allowing access to the presence of God was symbolically torn open.

Remember that when you go into the temple, symbolically speaking, you pass through the veil into the presence of

God. Christ and the Atonement are very much involved in the passing through the veil into the presence of God.

Concerning the veil, apostle and scholar Bruce R. McConkie wrote,

> Once each year in ancient Israel the high priest passed through the veil of the temple into the Holy of Holies. This solemn act was part of the sacrificial rites performed in similitude of the coming sacrifice of the Son of God, and these rites were performed for the remission of sins. (Leviticus 16) (Bruce R. McConkie, *Doctrinal New Testament Commentary*, 1:829)

Why did this happen only once a year? The Law of Moses dictated that the Day of Atonement was to be celebrated on a specific day only once per year. The Law of Moses was administered by the Levitical or Aaronic Priesthood. Under the Law of Moses, no priest held the higher or Melchizedek Priesthood. Therefore, no one was allowed to enter the Most Holy Place except the high priest, and even he was only allowed to enter only per year on the Day of Atonement. As those of you who have received your endowments know, the Aaronic Priesthood portion does not get you through the veil. Therefore, only the high priest, who was symbolic of Christ, got through the veil, and he only got in once per year on the Day of Atonement.

In his epistle to the Hebrews, Paul gave us great light concerning this issue:

> But into the second went the high priest alone, once every year, not without blood, which he offered for him himself, and for the errors of the people: The Holy Ghost this signifying, that the way into the holiest of all was not yet made manifest... But Christ being come an high priest of good things to come...entered in once into the holy place, having obtained eternal redemption for us... So Christ was once offered to bear the sins of many... Having therefore, brethren, boldness to enter into the Holiest by

the blood of Jesus, By a new and living way, which he hath consecrated for us, through the veil, that is to say, his flesh. (Hebrews 9:7-8, 11-12, 28; 10:19-20)

Here Paul teaches that the veil of the temple represents Christ's own flesh, and that none enter into God's presence without accessing the power of the Atonement, which includes the tearing of Christ's flesh.

Elder McConkie further explained,

But Christ is now sacrificed; the law is fulfilled; the Mosaic dispensation is dead; the fullness of the Gospel has come with all its light and power; and so—to dramatize in a way which all Jewry could recognize that the kingdom had been taken from them and given to others—Deity rent the veil of the temple 'from the top to the bottom.' The Holy of Holies is now open to all, and all, through the atoning blood of the Lamb, can now enter into the highest and holiest of all places, that kingdom where eternal life is found. Paul, in expressive language (Hebrews 9 and 10), shows how the ordinances performed through the veil of the ancient temple were in similitude of what Christ was to do, which he now having done, all men become eligible to pass through the veil into the presence of the Lord and to inherit full exaltation. (*Doctrinal New Testament Commentary,* 1:830)

The tearing of the veil when Christ died represented both the rejection of the priests who were in charge of the temple at that time, and opening up the presence of God to everybody who accepts the Atonement and receives the blessings and ordinances of the Melchizedek Priesthood.

The rending of the veil is also reminiscent of other scriptural descriptions of "tearing." People in the Bible and Book of Mormon would tear their clothes with anger and mourning. Perhaps God was also showing his anger and mourning when the veil was rent. The Ancients also rent their clothes when making covenants. Speaking symbolically, they would say something like, "If I break this covenant, may God tear me asunder, even as this cloth is torn asunder." The tearing of the bread in connection with the sacrament can also remind us of the tearing of the veil.

Summary

I hope that all of these things will help you have a greater appreciation for Christ and his Atonement. I hope you will see how shunning evil, fully accepting Christ in your life, repenting of your sins through the Atonement of Christ, and keeping your temple covenants will bring you into the presence of God where he stands ready to welcome you.

Discussion Questions

1. How can you recognize and identify priestcraft?
2. What can you do to be sure your are choosing Christ instead of priestcraft, robbers, and "Romans" in your own life?
3. How does the relationship between the Day of Atonement and the actual Atonement apply to your life?
4. What is the symbolism associated with passing through the veil?